READWELL'S

LEAR
IN A

**Easy Method of Learning Hindi
Through English Without a Teacher**

By :
ISHWAR DATT
M.A.

Readwell Publications
NEW DELHI-110008

Published by :
READWELL PUBLICATIONS
B-8, Rattan Jyoti, 18, Rajendra Place
New Delhi-110 008 (INDIA)
Phone : 25737448, 25712649, 25721761
Fax : 91-11-25812385
E-mail : readwell@sify.com
newlight@vsnl.net

© All Rights including subject-matter, style are reserved with the Publisher.

ISBN 81-87782-00-5

Printed at : Arya Offset Press, New Delhi.

Contents

Lessons			Page
1. Alphabets, Vowels			11
2. Consonants,			13
3. Vowels & Consonants put together			19
4. Building the Words			22
5. Introducing Conjuncts			30
6. Grammar		Noun	39
7.	,,	Gender	42
8.	,,	Number	54
9.	,,	Case	61
10.	,,	Pronouns	74
11.	,,	Verb	81
12.	,,	Tense	89
13.	,,	Auxiliary Verbs	109
14.	,,	Compound Verbs	113
15.	,,	Participles	116
16.	,,	Moods	120
17.	,,	Adverb	126

18.	Grammar Pronoun	128
19.	,, Adjective	133
20.	Imperatives & Useful Expressions	144
21.	Use of 'No'	153
22.	Interrogatives	156
23.	Some More Expressions —About the Shop	162
24.	Seasons & Weather	164
25.	Time	166
26.	Requests & Permissions	168
27.	Apologies	169
28.	Exercises for Letters Reading	171
29.	Conversation	178
30.	Translation	183
	Vocabulary	188

Preface

Sometimes ago while I was in search of a book on a science subject I chanced to see a book about which loud claims of learning a language in a short time without the aid of a teacher, were made. My curiosity knew no bounds and I wondered if it was possible to verify those claims. After reading a few pages here and there it took me no time to realise that this was a case of over-estimation—not that this could not be done but because the book had many drawbacks. However, it prompted me to create a work myself which should be worthwhile and should really benefit the learner. Although I will not claim that one can master a language in a given period of time because language is a boundless thing, yet I have taken care to present my work in a simple and easy-to-understand manner. A beginner can follow the lessons without any pause and realise that this language is just not that difficult to learn as he had dreaded.

There are writers who ignore grammar and fill their books with translated sentences in the pious belief that one can learn a language with the aid of only ready-made sentences. But this is wrong. Knowledge of grammar is essential for learning correct language. The superstructure of translations, howsoever well-mastered, just disappears as soon as the learner is asked to write grammatically correct sentences. The learner realises that he is nowhere near the language, and that the learning of grammar is basic to the learning of correct language. Once he understands the rules of grammar he has crossed more than half the way towards the learning of the language and easy presentation of these rules smoothens his further path.

—*Authors*

Readwell's Widely Read Books

LANGUAGE SERIES

RW-1	Learn English through Hindi
RW-2	Learn Hindi through English
RW-3	Learn Marathi through English
RW-4	Learn Gujarati through English
RW-5	Learn Tamil through English
RW-6	Learn Bengali through English
RW-7	Learn Assamese through English
RW-8	Learn Oriya through English
RW-9	Learn Telugu through English
RW-10	Learn Malayalam through English
RW-11	Learn Urdu through English
RW-12	Learn Kannada through English
RW-13	Learn Punjabi through English
RW-14	Learn French through English/Hindi
RW-15	Learn Arabic through English/Hindi
RW-16	Learn German through English/Hindi
RW-17	Learn Spanish through English
RW-18	Learn Nepali through English
RW-19	Learn Russian through English
RW-20	Learn Italian through English
RW-21	Learn Japanese through English
RW-22	Arabic for Beginners

DICTIONARIES

RW-23	Hindi-English
RW-24	English-Tamil
RW-25	English-Malayalam
RW-26	English-Telugu
RW-27	Marathi-English (Two-colour)
RW-28	English-Hindi (Pocket) (Two-colour)
RW-29	English-Bengali (Pocket) (Two-colour)
RW-30	English-Gujarati (Pocket) (Two-colour)
RW-31	English-English

FORMULAS

- Maths
- Physics
- Chemistry
- Science
- Biology

READWELL PUBLICATIONS

B-8, Rattan Jyoti, 18, Rajendra Place
New Delhi-110 008 (INDIA)
Phone : 5737448, 5712649, 5721761; Fax : 91-11-5812385
E-mail : readwell@sify.com
newlight@vsnl.net

BOOKS FOR EVERYONE

ENGLISH IMPROVEMENT

- N-128 Grammar & Composition
- N-241 General English
- N-249 20 Days to English Vocabulary
- N-273 Better English
- N-280 How to Write Effective English
- N-330 Words often Confused
- N-336 Spoken English
- N-338 A to Z Quotations
- N-339 A to Z Idioms and Phrases
- N-340 A to Z Proverbs
- N-341 A to Z Synonyms and Antonyms
- N-351 Basic English Grammar for Schools
- N-355 Correct English Usage
- N-354 Dictionary of Idioms and Phrases
- N-362 Dictionary of Quotations
- N-363 Instant Vocabulary Builder
- N-376 Dictionary of Synonyms & Antonyms

ESSAY WRITING

- N-343 School Essays, Letters and Paragraphs
- N-361 School Essays, Letters (For Juniors)
- N-344 136 Essays for College and Competitive Exams
- N-365 Advanced Essays for College and Competitive Exams

LETTER WRITING

- N-2 Applications for Better Jobs
- N-3 Business Letters
- N-6 Selected Letters
- N-10 Love Letters
- N-45 Top Every Day Letters
- N-79 1111 Letters for All Occasions
- N-274 How to Write Better Letters
- N-317 Perfect Letter Writer
- N-327 Model Business Letters
- N-331 Dynamic Letters
- N-332 Superb Business Letters

QUIZ BOOKS

- N-345 G.K. Quiz
- N-346 India Quiz
- N-347 Sports Quiz
- N-348 Geography Quiz
- N-353 Science Quiz
- N-357 Computer Quiz
- N-370 The World Firsts

G.K., CURRENT AFFAIRS & I.Q.

- N-26 G.K. & Current Affairs
- N-377 Handbook of G.K.
- N-77 Encyclopaedia of G.K.
- N-304 General Intelligence for Students
- N-334 सामान्य ज्ञान

NEW LIGHT PUBLISHERS

B-8, Rattan Jyoti, 18, Rajendra Place,
New Delhi-110 008 (INDIA)
Phone : 5737448, 5712649; Fax : 91-11-5812385
E-mail : newlight@vsnl.net

Vowels

अ आ इ
ई उ ऊ
ऋ ए ऐ
ओ औ अं
अः

Consonants

क	ख	ग	घ
ङ	च	छ	ज
ञ	ज	ट	ठ
झ	ढ	ण	त
ड	द	ध	न
थ	फ	ब	भ
प	फ	र	ळ
म	य	र	स
य	श	ष	ह
ह	ष	ज्ञ	ज्ञ

LESSON 1

Alphabets

(वर्ण माला)

First of all we will deal with vowels which number 11. Vowels are called 'swar' (स्वर) in Hindi :

अ (short) a — sounds like short 'a' as in 'at'
आ (long) aa — sounds like long 'aa' as in 'father'
इ (short) i — sounds like short 'i' as in 'it'
ई (long) i — sounds like long 'i' as in feet
उ (short) u — sounds like short 'u' as in 'bull'
ऊ (long) u — sounds like long 'u' as in cool
ऋ (short) ri — sounds like short 'ri' as in 'rib'
ए (long) aı — sounds like 'a' as in 'bay' 'say'
ऐ (diphthong) ai oi, — sounds like 'ai' as in 'ha' 'as'
ओ (long) o — sounds like 'o' as in 'coal', mole
औ (diphthong) ou, au — sounds like 'au' as in 'mouse' 'tout'

Other forms or signs of vowels (स्वर चिन्ह)
अ - no other form ; आ - T ; इ - f

ई - ी ;   उ - ◌ु ;   ऊ - ◌ू ;
ए - े ;   ऐ - ै ;
ओ - ो ;   औ - ौ ;   ऋ - ◌ृ

Note: short vowels are pronounced short and long vowels, long. अ (short) is inherent in every consonant sound but not written as such. We shall deal with this aspect of the letter later.

Exercise

Identify the following vowels and write their short forms also:

1. ऐ 2. आ 3. ई 4. ओ 5. अ
6. इ 7. ए 8. ऊ 9. औ 10. उ 11. ऋ

Ans.

1. 'ai' sounds as 'a' in the word 'cash' short sign ै
2. 'aa' as 'a' in 'father' short sign ा
3. 'i' as 'i' in 'Delhi' short sign ी
4. 'o' as 'o' in 'over' short sign ो
5. 'a' as 'a' in 'also' No short sign
6. 'i' as 'i' in 'sin' short sign ि
7. 'e' as 'a' in 'pet' short sign े
8. 'u' as 'u' in 'crook' short sign ू
9. 'au' as 'au' in 'out' short sign ौ
10. 'u' as 'u' in 'pull' short sign ु
11. ri as 'ri' in 'Rhesus' short sign ृ

The letters अ, आ, ओ, औ are also written like ऄ, ऑ, ॲ, ॳ respectively. We will deal with the placement of vowels, both in full or short form, later.

LESSON 2

Consonants

(व्यंजन)

There are thirtythree consonants in Hindi. In every consonant the short vowel sound of अ (a) is inherent but the letter itself is not used.

Consonant in Hindi	English equivalent	Hindi Sound
क (क्+अ)	K [Kit]	Ka
ख	Kh [Khud]	Kha [compound sound]
ग	g [gun]	ga
घ	gh [ghost]	gha [compound sound]
ड़	n [like n nasal—long	na
च	ch [chill]	cha
छ	chh [much]	chha [compound sound]
ज	j [jem]	ja

झ or झ़	jh [jheel] [no sound in English]	jha [compound sound]
ञ	na [half nasal] as in lunch	na
ट	t [take] hard	ta
ठ	tha [hard t]	tha [compound sound]
ड	d (hard) dog	da
ढ	dh [hard as dhal]	dha [compound sound]
ण	n [no English, hard sound]	na
त	t [soft as teeth] or t in French	ta
थ	th [soft as throat]	tha
द	d [soft as then]	da
ध	dh [as is dhow] Gandhi	dha [compound sound]
न	n [dental as neck	na
प	p [paper]	pa

14

फ	ph [photo]	pha
ब	b (bail)	ba
भ	bh [Bharat]	bha (compound sound)
म	m [more]	ma
य	y [year]	ya
र	r [roar]	ra
ल	l [lower]	la
व	v [vary, van]	va
श	sh [she]	sha
ष	sha [cerebral sound of sha-shut]	sha
स	s [sun]	sa
ह	h [her]	ha

As we have said above each of the consonants contains at the and vowel sound 'अ' but it is not written as such in full or short form. For example 'क' = (क+अ) but to write it like this is wrong. 'क' in itself gives the complete sound. However there are words which require 'क' to be written like क+अ, but in that case a sign (्) which is called हल् (hal) is attached to the consonant and the word is written like क्+अ= क; ख्+अ=ख; ह्+अ=ह

15

The consonant ग is an exception. in this case ग + अ = ग

Besides the above vowels and consonants, there are still some more alphabets in Hindi :

अं   अः   ँ   ड़   ढ़   ज़

अं is a nasal sound, like 'am' 'an', and is pronounced in Hindi as 'camp' 'cant' it is written in its full form or in short form. The short form is a mere full point placed over the consonant preceding it. For example कैंप, अबं, लंका (camp amb, Lanka)

अः sounds like the English 'ah' and is called 'visarga' in Hindi. This is also written in full or in short form which is a mere two vertical dots placed one above the other; for example कः (i.e in combination with a vowel it loses its written form) क + अः = (kah). In such letters the sound 'h' in 'ah' is not fully pronounced. Another example; 'पुनः' 'punah'

ँ sounds like the half nasal 'aun' in चांद chand (moon) दांत daunt. (tooth) This sign is used only when there is no vowel sign on top of a letter. For example दांत but मैं

ड़ does not have an exact sound in English. It gives a mixed sound in between the sound

16

of 'd' hard (as in doll) and (r) but it is read as 'r' as for example लड़ी (lari)

Similarly the letter ढ़. Its sound is also a mixture of dh (hard) and r but reads like rh as for example बाढ़ (barh=flood).

ज़ gives the sound of 'z'. This letter is no different from ज (j) in shape except for a dot placed under it.

There are yet three more letters in Hindi = क्ष, त्र, ज्ञ These three are a mixture of half sounds of two letters. They are called conjuncts.

क्ष represents the sounds of ख and य mixed together and is read as 'khya'. For example कक्षा (kakhya=class)

त्र represents the sounds of त and र mixed together and is read as 'tra'. For example छात्र (chhatra-student)

ज्ञ represents the sounds of, ग and य mixed together and is read as 'gya'. For example ज्ञान (gyan-knowledge)

Although these three letters are included in Hindi they are used not as frequently as in Sanskrit.

Exercise

Identify the following consonants:

1. ग	2. न	3. स	4. ज
5. क	6. घ	7. ड	8. भ
9. द	10. थ	11. ट	12. छ
13. च	14. त	15. ण	16. ह
17. ष	18. य	19. ल	20. ध
21. व	22. श	23. र	24. म
25. भ	26. फ	27. ख	28. ज
29. ध्र	30. ठ	31. ड	32. ढ
33. त्र	34. प	35. ब	36. ज्ञ
37. स	38. क्ष	39. ज	40. फ़
41. ढ			

LESSON 3

Vowels and Consonants put together

(स्वर तथा व्यंजन का मेल)

As already indicated अ (short) has no separate short form. Its sound is blended with the consonants. So we will take up the rest of the vowels one by one.

आ sounds like aa. Put together with consonants it is written as follows :

का (ka), खा (kha), घा (gha) and so on

The short form of आ is called akar (ा) It is always written *after* the consonants whose sound it affects.

इ sounds like i (short). In Hindi it is called ikar (ि). It is always written *before* the consonant whose sound it affects. For example कि (ki), खि (khi), बि (bi)

ई sounds like long (i) and is called iikar (ी) in Hindi. It is always written *after* the consonant whose sound it affects. For example की (ki), गी (gi), खी (khi)

उ sounds like u (short) and its short form is called ukar (ु). It is always written *below* but joining the letter whose sound it affects. For example कुन (kun), गुन (gun), खून (khun)

ऊ sounds like long u and its short form is called ukar (ू). It is also written *below* but joining the letter whose sound it affects. For example खून (khun), कून (kun).

ए sounds like long e and in its short form it is called ekar (`). It is written *above* but joining the letter whose sound it affects. For example लेट (late), डेट (date)

ऐ sounds like ai (diphthong) and in its short form it is called aikar (ˆ). It is written *above* but joining the letter whose sound it affects. For example : कैसा (kaisa), जैसा (jaisa).

ओ sounds like o and in its short form it is called okar (ो). It is written after the letter whose sound it affects. For example को (ko), लो (lo) Mark the difference between the short form of ए and that of ओ. In the case of the former, the above the letters is not accompanied by a horizontal line while the latter sign is joined to a horizontal line beneath it.

औ sounds like ou, au (diphthong) and its short form ˆ is called aukar. It is also written after the letter whose sound it affects. For example कौन (kaun), गौन (gaun). Here also the difference between the short form of ऐ and that of औ is similar as in the case of ए and ओ.

ऋ sounds like ri (short) and in its short form it is written like ृ under the letter whose sound it affects. For example नृप (narip= king).

Exercise

Identify the following :

कू, गो, लौ, खे, सु, मा, पि, नी, है, पृ, चो, घृ

21

LESSON 4

Building the words

(शब्द रचना)

After you have learnt the vowels and the consonants and begun identifying them, the next step is to build words using first two and then more alphabets in one word.

I

कान kaan (ear); खान khann (mine); गान gaan (song); बाल baal (hair); मान maan (respect); राग rag (song)

माला malaa (garland); ताला talaa (lock); नाना nanaa (grandfather); सारा saraa (whole)

गाना गा gaana ga (sing a song);

ताला लगा talaa laga (put a lock)

भाग जा bhag ja (run away)

गाना गा कर जा gaana ga kar ja (sing a song and go)

सारा काम करा कर जा Saara kaam kara kar ja (Go after helping all the work)

II

दिन din (day); हिम him (snow); नित nit (always); गिन gin (count); लिख likh (write);

मिल mill (meet), दिल dil (heart) इस is (this), इच्छा ichha (wish)

गिरि giri (hill) or (kernel), चिति chiti (heap), तिथि (date)

तिनका ला tinka la (bring the straw), तिरछा मत गिर tirchha mat gir (don't fall obliquely), तिमिर आता था timir aata tha (darkness was coming)

दाना मिला कर खा dana milla kar kha (Mix the grain and eat).

दादा गिरि गिनता था dada giri ginta tha (Grandfather counted kernals)

इसका काम सारा किया is ka kam sara kiya (did its whole work)

इधर रिमझिम बारश का मज़ा था idhar rimjhim barish ka maza tha (here the drizzle was enjoyable)

III

नीच neech (mean), नीर neer (water), भीड़ bheer (crowd), रीत reet (custom), पीत peet (yellow)

नीचता neechta (meanness), भीड़भाड़ bheer bhar (crowd), आपकी aapkee (yours), चीनी नहीं cheene naheen (no sugar)

आपकी चिट्ठी मिली aapki chithi milee (got your letter), सब्ज़ी खानी थी sabzi khani thi (had to eat vegetable), इस कार की चाबी किधर गई is kar ki chabi kidhar gayee (where is the key of this car), कीचड़ मत गिरा keechar mat gira (don't throw mud)

IV

रुकना rukna (to stay), झुकना jhukna (to bend), उधर udhar (thither), कुमारी kumari (maid or miss), मुल्क mulk (country), फुरसत fursat (leisure), कछुआ kachhua (tortoise), उठ uth (stand)

बड़ी वस्तु bari vastu (big thing), कुछ हिसाब रखती थी kuchh hisab rakhti thi (kept some account), तुम किस की याद रखती थी tum kiski yaad rakhti thee (who did you remember), मुझ सी अच्छी लड़की mujh see achhi larki (a good girl like me), फुफा तथा ससुर phupha tatha sasur (uncle and father-in-law) उधर जा udhar ja (go there)

V

बदबू badboo (bad smell), खुशबू khushboo (good smell), मूक mook (silent), मूसा moosa (rat), उल्लू ulloo (owl), ऊँट unt (camel).

चूहा भागा chooha bhaga (rat ran), खुशबू उड़ी khushboo uri (good smell spread), उल्लू उड़ा ulloo ura (owl flew).

चाकू किधर था ? chakoo kidhar tha ? (where was knife ?), ऊंचा पत्ता गिरा था uncha patta girta tha (high leave fell) सुनार उधर गया sunar udhar gaya (goldsmith went there), उसकी पुस्तक रखूंगा uski pustak rakhunga (will keep his book), ऊधम मत करना udham mat karna (don't make an uproar).

VI

एकता ekta (unity), एड़ी erhi (heel), केला keila (banana), लेना leina (take), क्लेश kaleish (quarrel), मेरा mera (mine), तेरे teire (yours)

एकता की शक्ति बहुत थी ekta ki shakti bahut thi (great strength in unity), तुझे किस से मिलाऊं? tujhe kis se milaon? (who would you meet)?, तारे मुझ पर हंसते थे tare mujh par hanste the (star laughed at me), तुम किस के साथ उधर गये? tum kis ke saath udhar gaye? (with whom did you go there?), तुम्हारी चाची का इधर से क्या काम ? tumhari chachi ka idhar se kiya kam? (what work your aunt has got hither?)

VII

ऐसा aisa (like this), पैसा paisa (paisa), मैं main (i), कैसा kaisa (how), बैल bael (ox), भैंसा bhaisa (he-buffalo)

पैसा मेरा है paisa mera hai (paisa is mine), भैंस दूध देती है bhains doodh deti hai (buffalo gives milk), मैं इस पेड़ पर बैठा main is per par baitha (I sat on this tree), मैं नदी में तैरा main nadi mein taira (I swam in the river).

मुझे उसकी तैयारी से ऐसा महसूस हुआ mujhe uski tayari se aisa mehsoos hua (with his preparation I felt like this), बैंक में चैंक ले जा रहा हूं bank mein check le ja raha hun (taking the cheque to bank), दैनिक काम इतनी देर से नहीं करना है dainik kam itni der se nahin karna hai (daily work should not be done so late)

VIII

दोष dosh (harm), कोष kosh (treasure), चोर chor (thief), ज़ोर zor (power), ओस oas (dew), आओ aaoe (come), खरगोश khargosh (hare), लोग log (people), गोल gol (goal).

कुछ काम करो kuchh kam karo (do some work), शोर करोगे तो मार पड़ेगी shor karoge to mar paregi (if you make a noise you will be punished), खेल कूद में सारा समय इसी तरह न बिताओ khel kud mein sara samay isi taraha na bitaau (Don't pass all the time in play like this), जब रामू ने किताब खोली तो वह बोलने लगा jab Ramu ne kitab kholi to woh boalne laga (when

Ramu opened the book then he began speaking),

IX

सौ sau (hundred), नौ nau (nine), मौत maut (death), औरत aurat (woman), चौअन chauan (fiftyfour), कौआ koua (crow), मौसम mausam (weather), और aur (and).

मौसेरी बहन mauseri bahen (daughter of mother's sister), उसकी बदौलत किसको पूछा गया है uski badaulat kisko poochha gaya hay? (who has been cared for due to him?), नौकर और नहीं मिले तो मैं किधर जाऊं naukar aur nahin mile to main kidhar jaaon? (If no other servant is available what can I do?), हौज़ में पानी कौन भरेगा hauz mein pani kaun bharega (who will fill the tank with water?), लौट कर उसने देखा कि कौन आ रहा था laut kar usne dekha keh kaun aa raha tha (he turned back and saw who was coming), कौआ रोटी का कौर लेकर उड़ा kaua roti ka kaur le kar ura (the crow flew with a piece of bread).

X

अं रंग rang (colour), रंक rank (beggar), घंटा ghanta (hour), बसंत basant (spring), बूंद boond (drop), आरंभ aarambh (beginning), निरंतर

nirantar (continuous), ननद nannad (sister-in-law), नंबर number (number), धौंस dhauns (threat).

XI

अः दुःख duhkh (sorrow), पुनः punah (again).

The अः is used in Hindi rarely. Its use in Sanskrit is widespread.

XII

ऋः ऋण rirran (debt), ऋतु ritu (season), ऋषि rishi (sage), ऋग्वेद Rigved (Rigved), ऋणी rini (debtor):

Exercises

Read the following sentences :

१ मुझे तीन दिन से जुकाम था
२ अब तुम कैसे हो ?
३ हमारे स्कूल का पुस्तकालय इधर है
४ कुछ दिन पहले तुम्हारा पत्र मिला
५ इतनी जल्दी सब आम खा लिए ?
६ इस घर में मेरे भाई का एक और दोस्त रहता है
७ मैं अपनी आंखों से यह देखना चाहता हूं
८ कोई कोई ऐसा कहा करते है ।

Ans :

1) mujhe teen din se zukam hai (I have been having bad cold for three days.)

2) ab tum kaise ho ? (how are you now ?)

3 hamare skool ka pustkalay idhar hai (our school library is on this side).

4 kuchh din pahle tumhara patr mila (got your letter some days ago).

5 itni jaldi sab aam kha liye ?
(eaten all mangoes so quickly).

6 is ghar mein mere bhai ka ek aur dost rahta hai (in this house lives another friend of my brother).

7 mein apni ankhun se yeh dekhna chahta hun (I want to see all this with my own eyes).

8 koi koi aisa kaha karte hain (some people say like this).

LESSON 5

Introducing Conjuncts

संयुक्ताक्षर (Samyuktakhar)

We have already discussed three Hindi conjuncts—क्ष, ज्ञ, त्र. In their case the two letters mixing together are different. In Hindi there are several consonants which are themselves doubled or trebled to produce a single sound. We shall deal with them below:

To double a consonant it is essential that the consonant written first should be halved. There are two ways to do this by writing it half or by writing it full and then placing a sign (्) हल् (hal) underneath it. For example

क+क is written as क्क or क्‌क

You will see that in this case the loop of the first letter (क) has been halved and then the half (क्) combined with the succeeding full क. In the other case the first क has been written in full but the हल् sign has been appended to it which means that this letter has been halved. In this case there is no need for writing the first क very close to the second क or for combining the two. This is true of

all letters which do not end in a horizontal line.

Other examples :

द+द is to be written as द्+द or द्द (dda)
त+त ,, as त्+त or त्त or त्त (tta)
च+च ,, as च्+च or च्च or च्चा (chcha)

In Hindi there are consonants which end in a separate horizontal line and which do not end in such a line. In the above examples the horizontal end-line is inherent but in alphabets like 'ग' there is a separate horizontal line-ending. When we have to double such alphabets the method is to drop the horizontal line of the first alphabet and write it very close to the succeeding alphabet. For example

ग+ग= ग्ग or ग्+ग
श+श= श्श or श्+श

In all cases of conjunction the vertical line of the first alphabet is dropped and the halved letter is brought under the vertical line of the succeeding alphabet,

In certain cases it is not the first alphabet which is halved when combining with the succeeding alphabet, but the second. For example :

त् + र = त्र or त्र (tra)
प् + र = प् + र् or प्र (pra)

This is mainly true of र when it is the second alphabet. But when र is the first alphabet and it is required to combine it with the next alphabet, "र" completely loses its original shape. For example

र + क = र् + क = र्क in कर्म (karm = work)
र + ल = र् + ल = र्ल in गर्ल (girl)

There are still more forms of conjunct consonants :

क् + त = क्त as in वक्त (wakt time)
श् + र = श्र as in श्रम (shram labour)
ह् + य = ह्य as in ह्यात (hayat life)
ह् + म = ह्म as in अह्म (ahm I)
द् + य = द्य as in विद्या (vidya knowledge)

Some more examples of conjuncts :

क् + य = क्य (kiya-what)
क् + ख = क्ख as in मक्खी (makhi fly)
क् + त = क्त as in रक्त (rakt blood)
क् + र = क्र as in चक्र (chakra wheel)
क् + ल = क्ल as in क्लेश (kalesh quarrel)

32

क्+ष=क्ष as in क्षार (khyar salt)
क्+ख=क्ख as in मक्खन (makhan butter)
क्+र=क्र as in क्रम (karam chain, order)
ख्+त=ख्त as in तख़्त (takht throne)
द्+य=द्य as in खाद्य (khadya food)
ज्+र=ज्र as in वज्र (vajra lightening)
ख्+य=ख्य as in ख्यात (khyat famous)
ख्+र ख्र as in फख्र (fakhr pride)
ख्+म=ख्म as in जख्म (zakham wound)
ग्+य=ग्य as in भाग्य (bhagya fate)
ग्+न=ग्न as in लग्न (lagan devotion)
ग्+र=ग्र as in ग्रीस (Greece)
ग्+व=ग्व as in ग्वाला (gwala milkman)
घ्+न=घ्न as in विघ्न (vighan difficulty)
घ्+र=घ्र as in घ्राण (gharan nose)
च्+र=चृ as in चृत (gharit ghee)
च्+छ=च्छ as in कुच्छ (kuchh some)
च्+य=च्य as in च्यन (chayan gather)
ज+ञ=ज्ञ as in संज्ञा (sangya noun)
ज्+व=ज्व as in ज्वर (jawar fever)
ज्+य=ज्य as in राज्य (rajya kingdom)
त्+व=त्व as in ममत्व (mamatav motherhood)
त्+य=त्य as in त्याग (tayag sacrifice)
त्+त=त्त or त्त as in कुत्ता or कुत्ता (kuta dog)

33

प् + त = त्त or त्त as in पत्ता or पत्ता (pata leave of a tree)

त् + न = त्न as in यत्न (yatan trial)

त् + र = त्र or त्र as in पत्र (patar letter)

द् + द = द्द as in भद्दा (bhadda ugly)

द् + ध = द्ध as in शुद्ध (shuddh pure)

द् + म = द्म as in पद्म (padma lotus)

द् + र = द्र as in द्रव्य (draviya liquid)

द् + व = द्व as in द्वार (dwar gate)

द् + य = द्य as in खाद्य (khadya food)

ध् + र = ध्र as in धर्ती (dharti earth)

ध् + र = ध्रृ as in धृष्टराष्ट्र (Dhritrashtar name)

ध् + य = ध्य as in ध्यान (Dhayan meditation)

न् + र = नृ as in नृप (narip king)

न् + र = न्र as in नर्तकी (nartaki dancer)

न् + त = न्त as in अन्त (ant end)

न् + म = न्म as in जन्म (janam birth)

न् + न = न्न as in अन्न (ann grain)

प् + य = प्य as in प्यार (piyar love)

प् + र = प्र or पं as in प्रश्न (prashan question) or दर्पन (darpan mirror)

प् + ल = प्ल as in प्लव (palav leave of tree)

ब् + र = बं as in बर्तन (bartan pot)

ब्र as in ब्रह्मा (Brahma God)

ब् + य = ब्य as in ब्याज (biyaj interest)

म् + ब = म्ब as in लम्बा (lamba tall)

34

म्+भ=म्भ as in दम्भ (dambh show)
म्+ल=म्ल as in म्लान (malan dirty or sad)
म्+य=म्य as in म्यान (miyan sheath)
म्+ह=म्ह as in तुम्हारा (tumhara yours)
म्+र=म्र as in नम्र (namr mild)
म्+म=म्म as in अम्मा (amma mother)
ट्+ट=ट्ट as in टट्टी (tatti latrine)
ट्+न=ट्न as in टैंक (tank)
र्+म=र्म as in कर्म (karm duty)
श्+र=श्र as in मिश्र (Mishar a caste)
ट्+र=ट्र as in ट्रक (tarrak)
ट्+ठ=ट्ठ as in चिट्ठी (chithi letter)
ल्+य=ल्य as in कल्याण (kalyan welfare)
ल्+ल=ल्ला or ल्ल as in बिल्ली or लिल्ला (billi-cat)
र्+व=र्व as in वर्ग (varg square)
र्+क=र्क as in तर्क (tark argument)
र्+ग=र्ग as in दुर्ग (durg fort)
स्+म=स्म as in समस्त (samast complete)
स्+य=स्य as in स्याना (sayana wise)
ह्+व=ह्व as in आह्वान (aahwan to call)

Identify the following vowel-consonant and other combinations:

1 का	2 खो	3 मो	4 गी	5 लि
6 से	7 पे	8 सो	9 जो	10 टे
11 गि	12 हः	13 डा	14 ढो	15 रो

16 ले   17 सी   18 बू   19 चों   20 टि
21 धौ   22 मैं   23 पि   24 नु   25 लू
26 बे   27 क्व   28 म्ल   29 प्य   30 श्र
31 नि   32 है   33 सर्प   34 स्मा   35 बिं
36 ड़ी

Ans. 1 क+आ=का as in काम (kaam) work
2 ख+ओ=खो as in खोल (khol) open
3 म+आ=मौ as in मौत (maut) death
4 ग+ई=गी as in गीत (geet) song
5 ल+इ=लि as in लिख (likh) write
6 न+ए=ने as in नेक (nek) good
7 प+ऐ=पैं as in पैन (pen)
8 स+ओ=सो as in सोना (sona) sleep
9 ज+ओ=जो as in जो (jo) who, whoever, whatever
10 ट+ए=टे as in टेढ़ा (tehra) crooked
11 म+इ=मि as in मिल (mill) meet
12 न+अ:=न: as in पुन: (punaha) again
13 ड+आ=डा as in डाली (dali) branch of tree
14 ढ+ओ=ढो as in ढोल (dhol) drum
15 र+ई=री as in छुरी (chhuri) knife
16 ल+ऐ=लैं as in लैंस (Lais)
17 स+ई=सी as in कैसी (kaisi) how
18 ब+ऊ=बू as in कबूतर (kabootar) pigeon

36

19 चं + ओ = चों as in चोंच (chonch) beak
20 ट + इ = टि as in टिकट (ticket) ticket
21 ध + औ = धौ as in धौला (dhaola) white
22 भ + ऐं = भैं as in भैंस (bhains) buffalo
23 प + इ = पि as in पिता (pita) father
24 न + उ = नु as in नुसख़ा (nuskha) prescription
25 ल + ऊ = लू as in आलू (aaloo) potato
26 ब + ए = बे as in बेल (bail) creeper
27 क् + व = क्व as in क्वाली (kaawali)
28 म् + ल = म्ल as in म्लान (malaan) faded
29 प् + य = प्य as in प्यार (piyar) love
30 श् + र = श्र as in श्रेणी (shreni) class
31 न + इ = नि as in निकल (nikal) get out
32 ह + ऐ = है as है (nai) is
33 स + र = सं as in सर्प (sarp) snake
34 म् + म = म्म as in अम्मा (amma) mother
35 ब + इ = बि as in बिंदू (bindu) a drop
36 ड़ + ई = ड़ी as in घड़ी (gharri) watch

Certain Hindi letters such as क, ख, ग, ज, फ accompany a dot below them and are written as क़ ख़ ग़ ज़ फ़। Dot denotes Persian influence on Hindi which came through

37

Urdu. These letters will give the following sounds :

क़ (qua) as in क़ीमत (price)
ख़ (kkha) as in ख़ुशबू (good smell)
ग़ (gga) as in ग़लत (wrong)
ज़ (za) as in कमीज़ (shirt)
फ़ (fa) as in फ़साद (quarrel)

The dotted letters ड़ and ढ़ belong to Hindi proper.

LESSON 6

Grammar

(व्याकरण)

The aim of this chapter is to give a brief introduction of the Hindi grammar because to write correct language, the knowledge of the basic rules of grammar is essential. In fact the best method of learning grammar is to read and read books and know the correct language by direct method. Yet for the beginner something of a background is required to explain a little easily the rules and the exceptions in grammar.

The first thing to know in grammar is 'noun' since it is the most important part of speech. The other equally important part of speech is 'verb'. We shall deal with them one by one.

Noun (विशेष्य=Visheshya)

In Hindi there are five kinds of noun :

1. **Proper noun** (व्यक्तिवाचक विशेष्य vyakti vachak) : This is the name of a particular person, name or thing i.e. कृष्ण, दिल्ली, मेघदूत

2. **Common noun** (जातिवाचक विशेष्य jativachak): This is the name of any number of things in

the same class or kind. For example man (पुरुष), city (नगर), boy (लड़का), book (पुस्तक)

3. Collective noun (समुदायवाचक विशेष्य samudayavachak): This is the name of a number of persons, animals or things spoken as a whole. For example श्रेणी (class), भीड़ (bhir-crowd), सभा (sabha, assembly)

4. Material noun (द्रव्यवाचक विशेष्य draviyavachk). This is the name of some material as सोना (sona-gold), लोहा (loha-iron), पानी (pani-water)

8. Abstract noun (भाववाची विशेष्य bhavvachi): This is the name of a quality, action or state. For example सुन्दरता (sundarta-beauty), बचपन (bachpan-childhood) etc.

Abstract nouns are formed in three ways, the verbs, the objectives and the nouns can be turned into abstract nouns with the help of certain suffixes. For instance the verbs take अ, आ, ब आई suffixes and become abstract nouns.

Examples :

लड़ना (to fight) = लड़ाई (larai-fighting)
जीतना (to win) = जीत (jeet-victory)
हंसना (to laugh) = हंसी (hansi-laughter)
बुलाना (to call) = बुलावा (bulawa-calling)

The adjectives take पा, ता, ई as their suffixes to become abstract nouns.

Examples

लम्बा (tall) = लम्बाई (lambai = tallness)
बहादुर (brave) = बहादुरी (bahaduri = bravery)
गरीब (poor) = गरीबी (garibi = poverty)
मोटा (fat) = मोटापा (motapa = fatness)
कू्र (rude) = कू्रता (karoorta = rudeness)

The nouns take पन, ई, ता etc. as their suffixes to become abstract nouns.

Examples

बच्चा (child) = बच्चपन (bachpan = childhood)
शत्रु (enemy) = शत्रुता (shatruta = enmity)
चोर (thief) = चोरी (chori = theft)

LESSON 7

Gender

(लिंग)

In Hindi gender is very important. To write correct Hindi it is essential to have correct knowledge of the gender because the form of the noun or verb depends on the gender of the subject. The change in gender means a change in the form of verb, adjective etc. For instance

मेरा लड़का काला है (My son is black)
but मेरी लड़की काली है (My daughter is black)

There are two genders in Hindi—पुलिंग (pulling=masculine) and स्त्रीलिंग (striling=feminine).

To distinguish the gender there are certain rules but they are not the last word on it. There are numerous exceptions too. Still it is better to have some broad knowledge of the rules to get going into the intricacies of correct writing.

1. The animate objects take their gender on the basis of their well-known sex. For example

लड़का (boy) = masculine (पुलिंग)
लड़की (girl) = feminine (स्त्रीलिंग)

2. In the case of inanimate objects the gender is determined on the basis of their end-vowels. Generally nouns ending with the sounds of 'अ' or 'आ' are masculine and those ending with ि (i) or ी (ee) are feminine. For example :

रास्ता (rasta = passage) is masculine
पत्ता (pata = leaf) " "
but लकड़ी (lakri = wood) " feminine
हानि (hani = loss) " "

But these rules are flexible. There are many exceptions. Some inanimate objects ending with the ा, आ vowel sounds are feminine. For instance भिक्षा (bhiksha = alms) or किताब (kitab = book)

Similarly some inaminate objects ending with ि or ी vowel sounds are masculine. For instance

घी (ghee = clarified butter)

As such we have to depend on the form and meaning of the noun for determining its gender. However the following rules should be kept in mind :

1. Names of professions take masculine gender irrespective of their end-vowel-sounds. For example

धोबी (dhobi=washerman); मोची (mochi=cobbler)

2. The names of rivers are always feminine :

गंगा (Ganga), जमुना (Jamuna), तापती (Tapti)

3. The names of places are generally masculine :

पंजाब, दिल्ली, मद्रास

4. The names of hills, mountains, oceans, days and months are masculine :

हिमालय, एवरेस्ट, हिन्दमहांसागर, रविवार, ज्येष्ठ etc.

5. The names of metals are masculine :
सोना, सीसा, ताँबा
but चाँदी (chandi=silver) is an exception.

6. The names of jewels are masculine :
हीरा (heera=diamond), नीलम् (neelam=sapphire), पुखराज (pukhraj=topaz)
however मणि (mani=ruby) is feminine.

7. The names of planets are masculine :
चन्द्र (chandar=moon), सूर्य (surya=sun) etc.

44

However पृथ्वी (prithvi = earth) is feminine perhaps because we call it mother earth.

8. The names of stars are feminine :
स्वाती (Sawati), अश्विनी (Ashwini)

9. The divisions of time are masculine on the basis of their meaning :
दिन, घण्टा, वर्ष, महीना, पल, मिनट
but रात (रात्रि night), सुबह (प्रातः morning), संध्या evening, दोपहर noon, feminine

10. The name of trees are masculine :
नीम (neem), पीपल (peepal) etc.
but बेरी (beri), इमली (imli) are exceptions.

11. The names of languages are feminine ;
बंगला, पंजाबी, हिन्दी, तामिल

12. The names of liquids are masculine :
दूध (doodh = milk), तेल (tel = oil), दही (dahi = curd), पानी (pani = water)
but छाछ (chhachh = buttermilk) is feminine.

13. The names of cereals are masculine :
चावल (chaval = rice), जौ (jau = barley), चना (chana = gram)
but सरसों (sarson = mustard), मूंग (moong) etc. are feminine.

14. The names of spices are feminine :

सुपारी (supari=betelnut); दालचनी (dalchini=cinnamon); हल्दी (haldi=turmeric), इलायची (ilaichi=cardamom)

but जीरा (jeera=cuminseed), अदरक (adrak=ginger), कपूर (kapur=camphor), तेजपत्र (tejpatr=cassia) are masculine.

15. The names of foodstuffs are feminine:

रोटी (roti=bread), भाजी (bhaji=vegetable) दाल (dal=pulses), etc.

So far we have dealt with gender in relation to the meaning of the nouns. The other method is to determine gender in accordance with the form of the words.

As we have already said words ending in आ (aa) vowel sounds are masculine and those ending in ई (ee, i) are feminine. This is a broad rule to determine gender in accordance with the form of the words.

For instance कमरा (room), छाता (umbrella) are masculine and नदी (river), कुरसी (chair) are feminine. So are रानी (queen), दासी (maid servant) feminine and राजा (king), दास (servant) masculine.

Besides there are other forms of ending to determine gender.

1. Abstract nouns ending in पा, पन, आव, are masculine. For example मोटापा (fatness), बड़पन (greatness), बढ़ाव (advance)

Words ending in आब are masculine :

हिसाब (account), गुलाब (rose). But there are exceptions—शराब (wine) किताब (book). These two words have feminine gender.

2. Abstract nouns which end in त्व, त्य, र्य and ब etc. are masculine. For example :

पशुत्व (like animals), नृत्य (dance), सौन्दर्य (beauty), गौरव (pride).

3. Words ending in त्र, त, न, etc. are masculine :

For example पत्र (letter) मीत (friend), यत्न (attempt)

4. words ending in ि and ी are feminine- For example मति (brain), बुद्धि (intelligence). But there are exceptions e g. गिरी (mountain) is masculine.

Words like रानी (queen), टोपी (cap) etc are feminine but there are a few words with ी ending which are masculine. These are दही

47

(curd), घी (clarified butter) पानी (water), मोती (pearl) जी, (mind). These words have masculine gender.

5. Words ending in त are feminine :

रात (रात्रि) night, छत (roof), सूरत (appearance) but there are certain masculine words with the same ending. For example : देहात (village), दाँत (tooth)

6. Words ending in हट, वट are feminine. For example घबराहट (perplexion), सजावट (decoration)

7. Words ending in स, श न are feminine : For example प्यास (thirst), लाश (body) उलझन (perplexion).

8. Words in या are feminine :

दुनिया (world). लुटिया (tumbler)

There are however certain exceptions: देश (country) ताश (playing card), बांस (bamboo) are masculine.

As we have already said gender in Hindi is the most important question. The knowledge of correct gender is so essential that without it writing or speaking of correct Hindi is impossible, We, therefore, give a list of words with their genders to acquaint the beginners with the intricacies of the langnage. The beginner may at first feel confused with the plethora of rules and an equal number of exceptions. But this is just at the beginning stage. As one sets more and more familiar with the language, all rules are relegated to the background and the knowledge of gender remains at the tip of the reader's fingers. The only thing that counts most is concentration and ability to grasp the vocabulary which we expect the learners to possess.

Masculine	**Feminine**
बूढ़ा (old) (man)	बूढ़ा (old) (woman)
देव (god)	देवी (goddess)
दास (servant)	दासी (maidservant)
मौसा (uncle)	मौसी (aunt)
भांजा (nephew)	भांजी (niece)
घोड़ा (horse)	घोड़ी (mare)
कुत्ते (dog)	कुतिया (bitch)
चूहा (mouse)	चूहिया
बछड़ा (calf)	बछड़ी
मुर्गा (cock)	मुर्गी (hen)
लड़का (boy)	लड़की (girl)
शेर (lion)	शेरनी (lioness)
ऊंट (camel)	ऊंटनी (she-camel)
हाथी (elephant)	हथिनि (she-elephant)
नाई (barber)	नाईन (wife of barber)

Masculine	Feminine
धोबी (washerman)	धोबिन (washerwoman)
माली (gardener)	मालिन (female gardener)
पंडित (pandit)	पंडिताइन (wife of pandit)
मेहतर (sweeper)	मेहतरानी (sweepress)
लोहार (blacksmith)	लोहारिन (wife of...)
भैंसा (he-buffalo)	भैंस (buffalo)
भेड़ा (ram)	भेड़ (sheep)
सुत (son)	सुता (daughter)
प्रिय (dear)	प्रिया (dear for female)
शिक्षक (teacher)	शिक्षिका (teachress)
नायक (actor)	नायिका (actress)
सम्पादिक (editor)	सम्पादिका (editress)
लेखक (writer)	लेखिका (female writer)
पाठक (reader)	पाठिका (female reader)
ठाकुर (priest)	ठकुराइन (wife of...)
जुलाहा (weaver)	जुलाहिन (female weaver)
बाघ (tiger)	बाघिन (tigress)
सिंह (lion)	सिंहनी (lioness)

Some words undergo total change of form with the change in gender :

पुरुष (male)	स्त्री (female)
बाप (father)	माँ (mother)

देवर (husband's brother)	ननद (husband's sister)
ससुर (father-in-law)	सास (mother-in-law)
राजा (king)	रानी (queen)
दामाद (son-in-law)	बहू (daughter-in-law)
भाई (brother)	बहिन (sister)
पिता (father)	माता (mother)
पति (husband)	पत्नी (wife)
वर (bridegroom)	कन्या (bride)

The gender of the words denoting relationship depends on the gender of the relation:

चचेरा भाई (cousin, son of father's brother)	चचेरी बहिन (cousin, daughter of father's sister)
ममेरा भाई (cousin, son of mother's brother)	ममेरी बहिन (cousin, daughter of mother's brother)
नीला आकाश (blue sky)	चमकीली धूप (bright sunshine)
मीठा शर्बत (sweet syrup)	मीठी दवाई (sweet medicine)
खट्टा नीबूं (sour lemon)	खट्टी दही (sour curd)
अच्छा लड़का (good boy)	अच्छी लड़की (good girl)

नेरा भाई (my brother)	मेरी बहिन (my sister)
तेरा काम (your work)	तेरी पुस्तक (your book)
हरा घास (green grass)	हरी सब्जी (green vegetables)
ठंडा पानी (cold water)	ठंडी शराब (cold wine)
उसका भाई (his brother)	उसकी बहिन (his sister)

Other words essentially feminine :—

कोयल (cuckoo), लोमड़ी (fox), गिलहरी (squirrel), बतख़ (duck)

दरखास्त (application), उम्र (age), किताब पुस्तक, (book), पीठ (back), अदालत (court), भीड़ (crowd), हलचल (commotion), हालत (condition), आफ़त (danger), मौत (death), हार (defeat), आँख (eye), किफ़ायत (economy), ज़मीन (earth), जांच (enquiry), किस्मत (fate), तक़दीर (fate), बाढ़ (flood), अक्ल (intelligence), बर्फ़ (ice), आदत (habit), मदद (help), भूख (hunger), टांग (leg), मुहब्बत (love), चाल (movement), भूल (mistake), याद (memory), जरूरत (necessity), कसम (oath), तसबीर (picture), तारीफ़ (praise), जड़ (root), नींद (sleep), मोहर (seal), चाय (tea), चीज़ (thing), जीत (victory), कमर (waist), दौलत (wealth), शराब (wine), लहर (wave), छाछ (buttermilk),

दया (kindness), क्षमा (forgiveness), इच्छा (wish), प्रार्थना (prayer), हानि (loss), वृद्धि (growth), मिहराज (arch), मुसीबत (difficulty), मिलावट (adultration), सिलाई (stiching), आवश्यकता (need), सहायता (help), मित्रता (friendship), दुनिया (world), जलन (burning), प्यास (thirst), बकवास (nonsense), सड़क (road)

Masculine words :

ग्रन्थ (book), रास्ता (road) कपड़ा (cloth), पैसा गन्ना (price), (sugarcane), लोटा (lot), पेशाब (urine), जबाब (answer), जुलाब (purgative), मत (opinion), चित्र (picture), पतन (fall), गीत (song), कृत्य (duty), स्वास्थ्य (health), गिरि (mountain), पानी (water), धान (rice), सूत (thread), निकास (outlet).

Exercises

1. Change the gender of the following :
जुलाहिन, पण्डित, पुरुष, प्रिया, देवर, ममेरी बहिन, माता, लड़की

2. Identify the gender of the following :
नाक, राम, दिन, चांद, सूर्य, हिमालय, गंगा, अध्यापिका, प्यास, स्वास्थ्य, बदन

3. Correct the following :

१. अच्छी लडका	२. मीठा रोटी	३. झूठा औरत
४. चचेरी भाई	५. हाथी दौड़ती है	६. गाय खाता है
७. बाघिनी जाता है	८. बैल आती है	९. लड़की रोता है
१०. ससुर अच्छी है	११. पानी गिरती है	१२. चांद निकलती है
१३. गंगा बहता है	१४. इच्छा होता है	१५. घी खाती है ।

LESSON 8
Number
(वचन)

There are two numbers in Hindi—singular (एक वचन) and plural (बहुवचन). Here also there are no absolute rules for change from one number to the other, yet some broad guidelines are there for everyone to learn.

1. The masculine singular nouns ending in 'अ' sound do not change in plural. For example घर, पेड़, फल

एक घर (one house) ५०० घर (500 houses)
एक पेड़ (one tree) ५०० पेड़ (500 trees)
एक फल (one fruit) २ फल (two fruits)

2. The masculine singular nouns ending in 'आ' change into 'ए' in plural. For example :

एक घोड़ा (one horse) दो घोड़े (two horses)
एक लड़का (one boy)   दो लड़के (two boys)
एक गधा (one donkey) दो गधे (two donkeys)

3. The masculine singular nouns ending in इ [i] do not change in plural. For

example :

एक कवि (a poet)   दो कवि (two poets)
एक मुनि (a saint)   दो मुनि (two saints)

4. The masculine singular nouns ending in ई do not change in plural :

एक माली (one gardner)   दो माली (two gardners)
एक हाथी (one elephant) दो हाथी (two elephants)

5. The masculine singular nouns ending in उ, ऊ, sounds do not change in plural. For example :

एक गुरू (one priest)   दो गुरू (two priests)
एक साधु (one saint)   दो साधु (two saints)
एक आलू (one potato)   दो आलू (two potatoes)
एक भालू (one bear)   दो भालू (two bears)

In above cases when the masculine singular noun is oblique i.e. accompanied by 'ने' the plural is formed by a change in the end sound. For example :

(Singuler)   (plural)
घर ने   घरों ने
फल ने   फलों ने
कवि ने   कवियों ने
मुनि ने   मुनियों ने
माली ने   मालियों ने
हाथी ने   हाथियों ने
गुरु ने   गुरुओं ने
भालु ने   भालूओं ने

In the case of masculine singular nouns ending in 'आ' the change in the plural number occurs as follows :

(Singular)	(Plural)
घोड़ा—एक घोड़े ने	दो घोड़ों ने
लड़का—एक लड़के ने	दो लड़कों ने
गधा—एक गधे ते	दो गधों ने

Nouns ending in 'आ' but showing relationship do not undergo change in their plural numbers. For example :

(Singular)	(plural)
दादा ने	दादाओं ने (grandfathers)
चाचा ने	चाचाओं ने (uncles)
लाला ने	लालाओं ने
राजा ने	राजाओं ने

FEMININE

The feminine singular nouns ending in the vowel sounds 'a' or 'आ' do not change or change taking 'ऐ' sound in place of 'आ' and 'ीं' in the case of oblique plural forms. For example :

(Singular)	(plural)
बहिन ने	बहिनों ने
गाय	गायें
गाय ने	गायों ने
नाना ने (grandfather)	नानों ने

56

(Singular)	(Plural)
राजा ने (king)	राजाओं ने
वक्ताने (spaekar)	वक्ताओं ने
आंख ने (eye)	आंखों ने
रात नें (night)	रातों ने

1. वह लड़का भागता है woh larka bhagta hai
   That boy runs —singular
   वह लड़के भागते हैं woh larke bhagtei hain
   Those boys run —plural

2. एक औरत गाती है ek aurat gati hai
   One woman sings —S.
   (कई) औरतें गाती हैं kai aurtai gati hain
   many women sing —P.

3. नदी बहती है nadi behti hai
   The river flows —S.
   नदियां बहती हैं nadian behti hain
   The rivers flow —P,

4. मैं जाता हूं main jata hun
   I go —S.
   हम जाते हैं hum jate hain
   we go —P.

5. तू खाता है tu khata hai
   you eat —S.

तुम खाते हो tum khate ho
you eat —P.

6. चिड़िया उड़ती है chirya urti hai
the sparrow flies —S.

चिड़ियाँ उड़ती हैं chiryan urti hain
the sparrows fly —P.

As you might have noticed from the above examples, the verb undergoes changes with the change in the number of subject. मैं becomes हम, है changes into हैं, था changes into थे or थीं, तू changes into तुम, The third person वह does not change but the verb changes e. g. वह जाता है—वह जाते हैं।

Feminine singular nouns ending in आ [aa] are changed in their plural forms as follows :

माता (mother)   माताएं (mothers)
दवा (medicine)   दवाएं (medicines)

Those ending in इ [i] i sound :

तिथि (tithi=a lunar day) तिथियां (lunar days)
मलिका (malika=queen) मलिकाएं (queens)

Those ending in ी [ई] ee sound :

मोरी (mori=hole) मोरियां (holes)
घोड़ी (ghori=mare) घोड़ियां (mares)

नदी (nadi = river)   नदियां (rivers)
लड़की (larki = girl)   लड़कियां (girls)

Those ending in 'उ' 'u' sound :

वस्तु (vastu = thing)   वस्तुएं (things)
धातु (dhatu = metal)   धातुएं (metals)

Those ending in 'ऊ' 'oo' sound :

झाड़ू (jharoo = broom)   झाड़ुएं (brooms)
बहू (bahoo = daughter-in-law)   बहुएं (daughters-in-law)

Feminine singular nouns ending in 'या' sound change as follows :

खटिया (khatiya = cot)   खटियां (cots)
बिटिया (bitiya = daughter)   बिटियां (daughters)

We now give below a list of singular words with their plural numbers in order to acquaint the reader with more of the problem of numbers :

Singular	Plural
नीति (niti = policy)	नीतियां (policies)
लता (lata = creeper)	लताएं
माता (mata = mother)	माताएं
कथा (katha = story)	कथाएं
भालू ने (bhaloo)	भालुओं ने
कपड़ा (kapra = cloth)	कपड़े

59

Exercises

1. Give the plural form of the following :

   माता, दरिया, गाय, मति, खटिया, मुनि, साधू, हाथी, चाचा ने, गधा

2. Correct the following :

   फलों, गधों, मतिएँ अच्छे लड़का, तीन बहिन

LESSON 9

Case

(कारक—Karak)

A word which determines the relation of a noun or pronoun with the verb is called a 'case'. There are eight cases in Hindi :

1. Nominative case   कर्ताकारक   नें जैसे राम ने
   (kartakarak) only in the past tense when the verb is transitive

2. Objective case or accusative case   कर्मकारक (karamkarak)   का

3. Instrumental case   करणकारक (karankarak)   से (by, with)

4. Dative case   सम्प्रदान कारक (sampradan karak)   को (to)

5. Ablative case   अपादान कारक (appadan karak)   से (from)

6. Possessive case   सम्बन्धकारक (sambandh karak)   का, के, की (of)

7. Locative case   अधिकरण कारक   में (in)
(adhikaran   पे or
karak)   पर (on)
8. Vocative case   सम्बोधन कारक   हे, अजी, अरे
(sambodhan   (Oh, O)
karak)

Examples

१. कर्ताकारक (ने)

मैं ने रोटी खाई   I ate bread   Singular
हमने रोटी खाई   We ate bread   Plural
तूने रोटी खाई   You ate bread   S.
तुमने रोटी खाई   You ate bread   P.
उसने रोटी खाई   He/She ate bread   S.
उन्होंने रोटी खाई   They ate bread   P.

ने is used when the verb used is transitive except in verbs like बोलना (speak)=मैं बोला (I spoke), भूलना=मैं भूला (I forgot), बकना=मैं बका (I barked), लाना=मैं लाया (I brought) and *not* मैं ने बोला, मैं ने भूला, मैं ने बका, मैं ने लाया

२. कर्मकारक (का) : In this case generally the English 'to' in Hindi become 'ko' (को) eg.

(A) हम को (hum ko), (B) मुझ को (mujh ko), तुम को (tum ko). But these Hindi postpositions are not acceptable to the correct reader. Instead we say हमें and not हम को, मुझे and not मुझ को and तुम्हें, not तुमको

When the pronoun used is in first person singular i.e. मैं, we also do not say मैं को but मुझ को

मुझे (मुझ को) जाना है
mujhe (mujh ko) jana hai
I have to go   Singular

हमें (हम को) जाना है
hamain (ham ko) jana hai
we have to go   Plural

तुझे (तुझ को) जाना है
tujhe (tujh ko) jana hai
you have to go   S.

तुम्हें (तुम को=आप को) जाना है
tumehn (tum ko=aap ko) jana hai
you have to go   P.

उसे or उसको जाना है
usse or us ko jana hai
he/she has to go   S.

उन्हें or उनको जाना हैं
unhein or unko jana hai
they have to go   —P.

3 करणकारक (से) : with this case-ending, an action is done—'से' means 'by', 'with', 'through' etc.

गेंद **से** खेलो gaind se khelo
Play with the ball

पैर **से** चलो payar se chalo
walk on foot

मुझ **से** बात करो mujhse baat krao
talk to us   S.

हम **से** बात करो humse baat karo
take to us   P.

तुझ **से** कहता हूँ tujh se kehta hun
I say to you   S.

तुम **से** (आप **से**) कहता हूँ
(tum se (aap se) kehta hun
I say to you   P.

उस **से** बात करो uss se baat karo
talk to him   S,

उन **से** बात करो uss se baat karo
talk to them   P.

धीरे **से** चलो (धीरे चलो) dhire se challo
welk slowly (Adverbial sense)

4 संप्रदान कारक (को) (के लिए) for : This case indicates the person or thing for which a work

64

is done. को means (to). Its case-ending signs are के लिए (kai liye), के वास्ते (ke vaste) i.e. for.

बीमार को (के लिए) दवा जरूरी है
Beemar ke liye dawa zaroori hai
medicine is essential for the sick

बच्चे को (के वास्ते) गाड़ी चाहिए
bache ko (ke vaste) gari chahiye
the child needs train.

गरीब को (के लिए) रोटी दो
garib ko (ke liye) roti do
give bread to (for) the poor

मुझे (मुझको) मेरे लिए—पुस्तक लाओ
mujhe—mujh ko—more liye—pustak lao
bring me a book   Singular

हमें (हमको) हमारे लिए पुस्तक लाओ
hamein (hamko) hamare liye pustak lao
bring us the book—plural

तुझे (तुझको)—तेरे लिए—पुस्तक लाओ
tujhe (tujhko) tere liye pustak lao
bring you a book   S.

तुम्हें (तुमको) तुम्हारे, आपके लिए पुस्तक लाओ
tumehn (tumko) tumhare aap ke liye
    pustak lao
  bring you a book   P.

65

उसे (उसको) उसके लिए पुस्तक लाओ
usse (usko) usske liye pustak lao
bring him/her a book   S.

उन्हें (उनको) उनके लिए पुस्तक लाओ
unhen (unko) unke liye pustak lao
bring them a book   P.

5 अपादान कारक—से [from] : The oblative case is indicative of separation from or camparison with something. Its signs are from, since, than) :

मैं तुम से बड़ा हूँ
main tumse bara hun
I am older than you

पेड़ से पत्ता गिरता है
per se pata girta hai
A leaf falls from the tree

मुझे पांच रोज से बुखार है
mujhe panch roz se bukhar hai
I have been in fever for five days

छत से पानी गिरता है
chhatse pani girta hai
water falls from the roof

दवा चमच से पिओ
dawa chamach se piyo
take medicine with a spoon

आदमी से भगवान बड़ा है
admi se Bhagwan bara hai
God is greater than man

6 सम्बन्ध कारक (का, के, की) of : The possessive case shows the possession of something. In the first person रा, रे री are used in place of का के की।

इस पेड़ का फल मीठा है
iss per ka phal meetha hai
the frist of this tree is sweet

इस लेखक की पुस्तक अच्छी है
iss lekhak ki pustak achhi hai
this writer's book is good

उस के कपड़े फट गए
uss ke kapre phat gaye
his clothes were torn

A singular masculine noun takes का while a plural masculine noun take के. A feminine noun, singular or plural, takes की. All depends on the number and gender of the noun following. For example :

इस कमरे का दरवाजा खोलो
iss kamre ka darwaza kholo
open the door of this room

इस कमरे के दरवाजे खोलो
iss kamre ke darwaze kholo
open the doors of this room

इस कमरे की खिड़की खोलो
iss kamre ki khirki kholo
open the window of this room

इस कमरे की खिड़कियां खोलो
iss kamre ki khirkian kholo
open the windows of this room

मेरा (मुझका) लड़का पास हो गया
mera (mujhka) larka pass ho gaya
my son has got through   Sing. Mas. noun

मेरी (मुझकी) लड़की पास हो गई
mery (mujhki) larki pass ho gaye
my daughter has got through
                         Sing. Fem. noun

हमारा (हमका) लड़का पास हो गया
hamara (hamka) larka pass ho gaya
Our son has passed   S.M. noun

हमारे (हमके) लड़के पास हो गए
hamare (hamke) larke pass ho gaye
our sons have passed   P.M. noun

हमारी (हमकी) लड़कियां हो गईं
hamaree larkian pass ho gayein
our daughters have passed   P.F. noun

तेरा (तुमका) लड़का पास हो गया
tera (tumka) larka pass ho gaya
your son has passed   S.M. noun

तेरी (तुमकी) लड़की पास हो गई
teri (tumki) larki pass ho gayee
your daughter has passed   S.F. noun

तुम्हारे लड़के पास हो गए
tumhare larke pass ho gaye
your sons have passed   P.M. noun

तुम्हारी (तुमकी) लड़कियां पास हो गई
tumhari (tumki) larkiyan pass ho gayen
your daughters have passed   P.F. noun

तुम्हारी (आपकी = respectful way of addressing the third person)

उसकी लड़की पास हो गई
usski larki pass ho gayee
his daughter has passed   S.F. noun

उसका (उनका) लड़का पास हो गया
usska (unka) larka pass ho gaya
his son has passed   S.M. noun

उनके लड़के पास हो गये
unke larke pass ho gaye
their sons have passed   P.M. noun

उनकी लड़कियां पास हो गईं
unki larkiyan pass ho gayein
their daughters have passed   P.F. noun

We can say that in the possessive case the suffix changes according to the gender and number of the noun possessed.

क, की are used to express the value of a thing :

दस रुपये मीटर का कपड़ा
das rupai metre ka kapra
ten rupees a metre cloth

दो रुपये की सब्ज़ी
do rupaye ki sabzi
two rupees worth vegetables

के, रे are used to indicate relationship irrespective of the number and gender of the noun possessed :

नीला के दो भाई हैं
neela ke do bhai hain
Neela has two brothers

मेरे (मैं + रे) दो हाथ हैं
mere do hath hain
I have two hands

7. अधिकारण कारक : (में, पर) **in, on :**—This case denotes the place or time at which some action takes place. Its post-position or case-ending signs are में, पर

छत पर जाओ chhat par jaao
go on the roof

घर में बैठो ghar mein baitho
sit in the house

किताब मेज़ पर है kitab mez par hai
the book is on the table

उस जेब में क्या है?
uss jeb main kiya hai
what is in that pocket?

मुझ में, पर (mujh main, par)   Sing. Mas.

हम में, पर (ham main, par)
                        Plu. mas or fem.

तुम में, तुझ में (पर) (tum main, tujh main)
        (par)   S.M. or F.

आप में, पर (aap main, par)   P.M. or F.

उस में, पर (uss main, par)   S.M. or F.

उन में, पर (un main, par)   P.M. or F.

8. सम्बोधन कारक : This is the case of address and signifies the person addressed to.

Its signs are हे, अरे अजी, etc. These signs are used before the nouns addressed :

हे मित्र ! इतने दिन कहाँ रहे ?
hey mitr ! itne din kahan rahe ?
Oh friend! where were you all
  these days ?

हे भगवान ! यह क्या हो गया ?
hey Bhagwan ! yeh keya ho giya ?
Oh God ! what is all this ?

अरे भाई ! क्यों लड़ते हो ?
arei bhai ! kiyun larte ho
O brother ! why do you quarrel ?

अजी छोड़ो ! इसमें क्या रखा है ?
aji chhoro ! iss main kya rakha hai ?
O, leave it ! what is there in it ?

राम ! तुम कब आए ?
Ram ! tum kab aaye ?
Ram ! when did you come ?

Exercises

1. Fill in the gaps :
१. तुम———गाना गाया   २. राम———पुस्तक पढ़ी
३. सीता———पत्र लिखा   ४. तुम———क्या हुआ

५. मुझ——कहाँ जाना था ६. नीला—राम—शादी की
७. वह मुझ——डरता है ८. ज़ोर——मत बोलो
९. गरीब——भिक्षा दो १०. पेड़ों——पत्ते गिरते हैं
११. सीता——चार भाई १२. उस——एक बाप
१३. मे……दो बहिनें १४. मे……एक भाई
१५. मैं इस घर——रहता हूं १६. गली——बहुत भीड़ है
१७. सड़क——बहुत भीड़ है
१८. ——भगवान ! मैं कहाँ जाऊँ ?

Ans.

१. ने	२. ने	३. ने	४. को
५. को (मुझे)	६. ने, से	७. से	८. से
९. को	१०. से	११. के	१२. का
१३. मेरी	१४. मेरा	१५. में	१६. में
१७. पर	१८. है		

2. Correct the following :

१. मुझ ने बोला २. लड़के ने बोला
३. तेरे भाई का बेटी ४. राम की हाथ से
५. मैं शाम में आऊंगा

Ans.

१. मैंने बोला २. लड़का बोला
३. तेरे भाई की बेटी ४. राम के हाथ से
५. मैं शाम को आऊंगा

LESSON 10
Pronouns
(सर्वनाम Sarvnam)

A pronoun is a word which is placed in place of a noun. Its gender and number depend on the noun it replaces. There are 11 pronouns in Hindi—मैं (I), तू (you), आप (yourself), यह (this), वह (that) जो (who or which), कुछ (anything), कौन (who or which) क्या (what), कोई (anyone, someone), सो or वह (he or that)

There are six kinds of pronouns:

1 Personal pronoun (पुरुषवाचक सर्वनाम): The personal pronouns are मैं (I) singular, हम, हम लोग (we, we people) plural, तू (you) singular, तुम, तुम लोग (you, you people) plural, वह (he) singular, वे (they) plural, यह (this) singular, ये (these) plural, वे (he-respectful) singular, वे लोग (they) plural.

Examples :

मैं जाता हूँ
main jata hun = I go   Singular

हम जाते हैं
hum jate hain = we go   Plural

तू जाता है
(tu jata hai = you go   S,

तुम or तुम लोग जाते हो
tu or tum log jate ho = you go   S.

आप जाते हैं
aap jate hain = you go S. respectfully

आप लोग जाते हैं
aap log jate hain = all of you go   P.

वह जाता है
woh jata hai = he goes   S.

वे जाते हैं
way jate hain = they go   P.

यह आदमी जाता है
yeh admi jata hai = this man goes   S.

ये जाते हैं
yeh jate hain = these people go   P,

वे लोग जाते हैं
way log jate hain = those people go P.

2 Relative pronoun (सम्बन्धबाचक सर्वनाम) : Its signs are जो, सो. This pronoun denotes relationship.

Exemples :

उस के पास जो पुस्तक है, सो मेरी है
uss ke pass jo pustak hai so meri hai
the book with him is mine

राम जो तुम्हारा मित्र है सो मेरे साथ खेलता है
Ram jo tumhara mitr hai so mere saath khelta hai
Ram who is your friend plays with me

3 **Reflexive pronoun** (स्वयंवाचक सर्वनाम) : In this category fall words like आप, स्वयं etc. These are used in all the three persons.

Examples

तुम आप (स्वयं) ही आ जाना
tum aap-soyam-hi aa jana
You come yourself

मैं आप (स्वयं) ही वहाँ जाऊँगा
main aap-soyam-hi wahan jaonga
I will go there myself

वह आप (स्वयं) ही वहां जाता था
woh aap-soyam-hi wahan jata tha
He himself used to go there

4 **Demonstrative pronoun** (संकेतवाचक सर्वनाम): This pronoun whose signs are यह, वह points to any particular person or thing.

Examples :

यह मेरा मकान है yeh mera makan hai
this is my house   S.

वह उसका घर है woh uska ghar hai
that is his her house   S.

ये मेरे बच्चे हैं [ye mere bache hain
these are my children   P,

वे उसकी पुस्तकें हैं
way uski pustkein hain
those are her/his books   P.

5 Interrogative pronoun (प्रश्नवाचक सर्वनाम) :
This pronoun has कौन, क्या signs and denotes questioning.

Examples

कौन आया ? (kaun aya = who came ?)
यह क्या है ? (yeh kiya hai = what is this?)

6 Definite and Indefinite pronouns (निश्चय तथा अनिश्चयवाचक सर्वनाम) : In this category fall signs like यह (singular) ये (plural); वह (singular) वे (plural), कोई, कुछ etc. The first two are used as Definite pronouns and the latter two as Indefinite pronouns.

Examples

यह मेरी पुस्तक है yeh meri pustak hai
this is my book   —thing near

ये मेरी पुस्तकें हैं ye meri pustkain hain
these are my books   —things near

वह कहाँ गया ? woh kahan gaya
where has he gone ?   —far off thing

वे कहां गएं ? way kahan gaye
where have they gone ?   —far off thing

कोई is used in different ways. It can **show unknown object**, express a sense of **approximation** etc.

Examples :

यहाँ कोई आया है
yahan koi aaya hai
somebody has come here —unknown

मैं वहां कोई एक घंटा बैठा
main wahan koi ek ghanta baitha
I sat there for about an hour
—approximate

यहां तो सब कोई जा सकता है
yahan to sab koi ja sakta hai
there all people can go —collective

यहाँ हर कोई आ सकता है
yahan har koi aa sakta hai
here everyone can come —collective

हमें सदा कोई न कोई काम करना पड़ता है
we have to do some or the other work always —optional

कुछ is sometimes used as a pronoun in the following sense :

यहाँ कुछ पुस्तकें पड़ी थी
yahan kuchh pustkain pari theen
here some books were lying

कुछ हमें भी तो सिखाओ
kuchh hamein bhi to sikhao
teach us something

Exercises

Indicate the pronouns in the following :

१. यह क्या है ?
२. कोई न कोई जायेगा ही
३. क्या खा रहे हो ?
४. जो सोता है सो खोता है
५. मैं स्वयं ही वहां जाऊंगा
६. वह कौन है ?
७. आप यहां कब आए ?
८. कौन जाता है ?
९. अंधेरे में कोई है
१०. सब कोई यह काम कर सकते हैं
११. गाड़ी कोई आध घंटा देर से आई
१२. यह उसकी गाय है
१३. कुछ न कुछ देना ही पड़ेगा
१४. कोई न कोई यह काम करेगा ही
१५. वे लोग कौन थे ?
१६. यह मेरी पुस्तक है ।

Ans :

1 personal	2 idefinite
3 interrogative	4 relative
5 reflexive	6 interrogative
7 personal	8 interrogative
9 indefinite	10 indefinite
11 indefinite	12 demonstrative
13 indefinite	14 indefinite
15 interrogative	16 demonstrative

LESSON 11

Verb

(क्रिया Kriya)

The verb is also an important part of speech in Hindi because it changes in its form in accordance with the gender of the subject, the number and person of the subject and in accordance with the tense and mood.

Examples

वह जाता है (woh jata hai = he geos)

वह जाती है (woh jati hai = she goes)

वे जाते हैं (way jate hain = they go)

मैं जाता हूं (main jata hun = I go)

तुम जाते हो (tum jate ho = you go)

वह जाता था (woh jata tha = he used to go)

वह जाएगा (woh jayega = he will go)

There are two kinds of verb :

Transitive and intransitive :

The transitive verb shows an action which is complete only with the help of an object :

वह खाता है (he eats, what ?) without know-ign the object teh sense of the sentence is incomplete. So we have to say

बह रोटी बाता है (he eats bread)

The intransitive verb shows an action which is complete even without the need of an object :

मैं दौड़ता हूं (I run), This sentence is in itself complete and requires no object.

The following is the list of some useful verbs :

To abuse	गाली देना
" accept	स्वीकार करना
" admire	तारीफ़ करना
" answer	जवाब देना
" approve	मंजूर करना
" arrive	पहुंचना
" ascend	चढ़ना
" ask	पूछना
" awake	जागना
" bathe	नहाना
" be	होना
" be afraid	डरना
" beat	पीटना

To become	होना
" begin	शुरू करना
" believe	विश्वास करना
" blame	दोष देना
" borrow	उधार लेना
" break	तोड़ना
" bring	लाना
" build	बनाना
" buy	खरीदना
" carry	उठाना
" change	बदलना
" chat	गप्प मारना
" choose	चुनना
" clean	साफ करना
" climb	चढ़ना
" come	आना
" compare	मुकाबला करना
" conceal	छुपाना
" consent	मंजूर करना
" continue	जारी रखना
" cook	पकाना
" cough	खांसी आना
" cover	ढकना
" cry	चिल्लाना
" cut	काटना
" dance	नाच करना

To	decide	फैसला करना
"	deny	इनकार करना
"	desire	इच्छा करना
"	die	मरना
"	dig	खोदना
"	dine	रोटी खाना
"	do	करना
"	doubt	संदेह करना
"	dream	स्वप्न देखना
"	drink	पीना
"	drive	गाड़ी चलाना, पशु हांकना
"	eat	खाना
"	excuse	क्षमा करना
"	expect	आशा रखना
"	fall	गिरना
"	fear	डरना
"	feed	खिलाना
"	fight	लड़ना
"	find	ढूंढना
"	finish	समाप्त करना
"	follow	पीछा करना
"	forget	भूलना
"	gain	लाभ उठाना
"	give	देना
"	go	जाना
"	grow	बढ़ना
"	hang	फांसी देना

To	hate	घृणा करना
"	hear	सुनना
"	hide	छुपाना
"	hire	किराये पर लेना
"	hold	पकड़ना
"	hope	आशा करना
"	imagine	कल्पना करना
"	inform	खबर करना
"	introduce	परिचय देना
"	invite	निमंत्रण देना
"	jump	कूदना
"	jeer	मजाक करना
"	keep	रखना
"	know	जानना
"	laugh	हंसना
"	learn	सीखना
"	lend	उधार देना
"	lie down	लेटना
"	live	रहना
"	light	रोशनी करना
"	like	पसंद करना
"	lose	खोना
"	love	प्यार करना
"	make	बनाना
"	marry	ब्याह करना
"	meet	मिलना

To mix	मिलाना
" mount	चढ़ना
" move	हिलना
" obey	आज्ञा मानना
" object	आपत्ति करना
" open	खोलना
" order	हुक्म करना
" play	खेलना
" please	प्रसन्न करना
" pluck	तोड़ना (फूल)
" praise	प्रशंसा करना
" prepare	तैयार करना
" prevent	रोकना
" print	छापना
" punish	दंड देना
" quarrel	लड़ना
" read	पढ़ना
" reap	काटना
" receive	स्वागत करना
" regret	खेद प्रकट करना
" remember	याद करना
" repair	मरम्मत करना
" rest	आराम करना
" rise	उठना
" run	दौड़ना
" say	कहना

" search	ढूंढना
" see	देखना
" sell	बेचना
" send	भेजना
" serve	सेवा करना
" sew	सिलाई करना
" shut	बंद करना
" sigh	ठंडी सांस लेना
" sign	हस्ताक्षर करना
" sing	गीत गाना
" sit	बैठना
" sleep	सोना
" smell	सूंघना
" sow	बीज बोना
" speak	बोलना
" spin	कातना, चक्कर लगाना
" spit	थूकना
" stay	रहना
" steal	चोरी करना
" strike	ठोकर लगाना
" study	पढ़ना
" swear	कसम खाना
" take	लेना
" taste	स्वाद लेना
" teach	शिक्षा देना
" tear	फाड़ना

To tell	बताना
" thank	धन्यवाद करना
" tie	बांधना
" touch	छूना
" translate	अनुवाद करना
" travel	यात्रा करना
" understand	समझना
" wash	धोना
" wake	जागना
" wait	प्रतीक्षा करना
" want	चाहना
" walk	चलना
" wear	पहनना
" weep	रोना
" weigh	तोलना
" work	काम करना
" worship	पूजा करना
" write	लिखना
" yawn	उबासी लेना, अंगड़ाई
" yell	चीखना

LESSON 12
Tense
(काल)

There are three tenses in grammar—present (वर्तमान काल=vartman kaal); past (भूतकाल=bhoot kaal) and future (भविष्यत् काल=bhavishayat kaal) The three tenses are further divided into many types.

Masculine 1st person singular

मैं खाता हूं (main khata hun=I eat)
  Present

मैं खाता था (main khata tha=I aet)
  Past

मैं खाऊंगा (main khaonga=I will eat)
  Future

Feminine 1st person singular

मैं खाती हूं (main khati hun=I eat) P.

मैं खाती थी (main khati thi=I ate)
  Past

मैं खाऊंगी (main khaongi=I will eat) F.

Masculine 2nd person singular

तू खाता है (tu khata hai=you eat) P.

तू खाता था (tu khata tha=you ate)
  Past

तू खाएगा (tu khayega = you will eat) F.

Feminine 2nd person singular

तू खाती है (tu khati hai = you eat) P.

तू खाती थी (tu khati hai = you ate) Past

तू खाएगी (tu khayegi = you will eat) F.

Masculine 3rd person singular

वह खाता है (woh khata hai = he eats) P.

वह खाता था (woh khata tha = he ate) Past

वह खाएगा (woh khayega = he will eat) F.

Feminine 3rd person singular

वह खाती है (woh khati hai = she eats) P.

वह खाती थी (woh khati thi = she ate) Past

वह खाएगी (woh khayegi = she will eat) F.

Sub-divisions of Tenses

Present—Present Indefinite, present doubtful, present continuous

Past —Past indefinite, present perfect, past perfect, past imperfect continuous, past doubtful, past conditional

Future—Future indefinite, future doubtful.

As we have said already the verb in Hindi changes in accordance with the gender, number and person of the nominative. We shall deal with this most important aspect in detail now :

Present Tense (वर्तमान काल)

मैं खाना खाता हूं main khana khata hun
I eat bread   first person mas. sing.

हम खाना खाते हैं ham khana khate hain
we eat bread   first per. mas. plu.

तू खाना खाता है tu khana khata hai
you eat bread   second per. mas. sing.

आप (तुम) खाना खाते हो aap (tum) khana khate ho
you eat bread   second per. mas. plu.

वह खाना खाता है woh khana khata hai
he eats food   third per. mas. sing.

वे खाना खाते हैं way khana khate hain
they eat bread   third per. mas. plu.

Change of gender

मैं खाना खाती हूं main khana khati huni
I eat bread   first p. fem. sin.

हम खाना खाती है ham khana khati han
we eat bread   first p. fem. plu.

तू खाना खाती है tu khana khati hai
you eat bread   second p. fem. sin.

आप (तुम) खाना खाती है aap (tum) khana khati hain
yon eat bread   second p. fem. plu.

बह खाना खाती है woh khana khati hain
she eats bread   third p. fem. sin.

वे खाना खाती हैं way khana khti hain
they eat bread   third p. fem. plu.

Changes of Tenses
Past Tense (भूतकाल)

मैंने खाना खाया maine khana khaya
I ate bread

हमने खाना खाया hamne khana khaya
we ate bread

तूने खाना खाया tune khana khaya
you ate bread

तुमने खाना खाया tumne khana khaya
you ate bread

उसने खाना खाया ussne knana khaya
he ate bread

उन्होंने खाना खाया unhun ne khana khaya
they ate bread

Future Tense (भविष्यत काल)

मैं खाना खऊँगा main khana khaunga
I shall eat bread

हम खाना खाएँगे ham khana khange
we shall eat bread

तुम खाना खाओगे tum khana khaoge
you will eat bread

वह खाना खाएगा woh khana khayega
he will eat bread

वे खाना खाएँगे way khana khayenge
they will eat bread

We now give a few examples of verbs in all the three tenses:

Present	Past	Future
see = देखना (dekhna)	देखा (dekha)	देखेगा (dekhega)
eat = खाना (khana)	खाया (khaya)	खाएगा (khayega)
drink = पीना (peena)	पिया (piya)	पियेगा (piyega)
sleep = सोना (sona)	सोया (soya)	सोयेगा (soyega)
rose = उठना (utthna)	उठा (uttha)	उठेगा (utthega)
talk = बोलना (bolna)	बोला (bola)	बोलेगा (bolega)
write = लिखना (likhna)	लिखा (likha)	लिखेगा (likhega)
bathe = नहाना (nahana)	नहाया (nahaya)	नहायेगा (nahayege)

Present indefinite tense (सामान्य वर्तमान काल)

मैं जाता हूं, हम जाते हैं, तू जाता है, तुम जाते हो, वह जाता है, वे जाते हैं—all are examples of this tense in masculine singular and plural number and in all three persons. When feminine gender is required the verb 'जाता' is changed into 'जाती' ।

Present Continuous Tense
(तात्कालिक वर्तमान काल)

मैं जा रहा हूं main ja raha hun
I am going

हम जा रहे हैं ham ja rahe hain
we are going

तू जा रहा है tu ja raha hai
you are going

तुम जा रहे हो tum ja rahe ho
you are going

वह जा रहा है woh ja raha hai
he is going

वे जा रहे हैं way ja rahe hain
they are going

Doubtful Present Tense (सन्दिग्ध वर्तमान काल) :

मैं जाता हूंगा main jata hoonga
I may be going   Masculine

मैं जाती हूंगी main jati hoongi
I may be going   Feminine

हम जाते हूंगे ham jate hoonge
we may be going   M.

हम जाती हूंगी ham jati hoongi
we may be going   F.

तू जाता होगा tu jata hoga
you may be going   M.

तू जाती होगी tu jati hogi
you may be going   F.

तुम जाते होगे tum jate hoge
you may be going   M.

तुम जाती होगी tum jati hogi
you may be going   F.

वह जाता होगा woh jata hoga
he may be going   M.

वह जाती होगी woh jati hogi
she may be going   F.

वे जाते होंगे way jate hoonge
they may be going   M.

वे जाती होंगी way jati hoongi
they may be going   F.

95

Past Tense (भूत काल) Bhoot kaal :

There are six kinds of past tense in Hindi

(I) Past Indefinite Tense (सामान्य भूत)
   (Samanya bhoot)

Past Indefinite tense in formed by adding अ-ए-ई to the root of the verb.

Examples

Root verb = खेल

मैं खेला   main khela = I played
  first person sin. mas.

हम खेले   ham khele = we played
  first per. plu. mas.

मैं खेली   main kheli = I played
  first per. sin. feminine

हम खेलीं   ham khelin = we played
  first per. plu. feminine

तू खेला   tu khela = you played
  second per. sin. mas.

तुम खेले   tum khele = you played
  second per. plu. mas.

तू खेली   tu kheli = you played
  2nd p. sin. fem.

तुम खेलीं tum khelein = you played
  2nd p. plu. fem.

वह खेला woh khela = he played

3rd p. sin. mas.

वे खेले woh khele = they played

3rd p. plu. mas.

वह खेली woh kheli = she played

3rd p. sin. fem.

वे खेलीं way khelen = they played

3rd p. plu. fem.

[II] Present perfect (श्रासन्न भूत) Aasanbhoot

This tense is formed by adding the present tense of the verbs 'to be' (होना) to the Past Indefinite tense. For example :

मैं गया हूं main gaya hun = I have gone

1st p. sin. mas.

मैं गई हूं main gayee hun = I have gone

1st p. sin. fem.

हम गए हैं hum gaye hain = we have gone

1st p. plu. mas.

हम गईं हैं hum gayee hain = we have gone

1st p. plu. fem.

तू हंसा है tu hansa hai = you have laughed

2nd p. sin. mas.

तू हंसी है tu hansi hai = you have laughed

2nd p. sin. fem.

तुम हंसे हो tum hanse ho = you have laughed
2nd p. plu. mas.

तुम हंसी हो tum hansi ho = you have laughed
2nd p. plu. fem.

वह गया है woh gaya hai = ne has gone
3rd p. sing. mas.

वे गए हैं way gaye hain = they have gone
3rd p plu. mas.

वह गई है woh gayee hai = she has gone
3rd p. sin, fem.

वे गई हैं way gayee hain = they have gone
3rd p. plu. fem.

[III] Past Perfect (पूर्ण भूतकाल poorn bhootkal)

When the past tense of the verbs 'होना' is added to the Past Indefinite tense, it becomes Past Perfect. Examples:

मैं गया था main gaya tha
I had gone   1st per. sin. mas.

मैं गई थी main gayee thi
I had gone   ,,   ,,   fem.

हम गए थे ham gaye thay
we had gone   ,,   plu. mas.

हम गई थीं ham gayee theen
we had gone   ,,   ,,   fem.

तू गया था tu gaya tha
you had gone   2nd per. sin. mas.

तू गई थी tu gayee thi
you had gone   ,,   ,,   fem.

तुम गए थे tum gaye thay
you had gone   ,,   plu. mas.

तुम गई थीं tum gayee thin
you had gone   ,,   ,,   fem.

यह गया था woh gaya tha
he had gone   3rd sin. mas.

वह गई थी woh gaye thi
she had gone   ,,   ,,   fem.

वे गए थे way gaye thay
they had gone   ,,   plu. mas.

वे गई थीं way gaye theen
they had gone   ,,   ,,   fem.

[IV] Past doubtful
(सन्दिग्ध भूतकाल) Sandigadh bootkal

This tense is formed by the addition of the future tense of the verb 'होना' to the Past Indefinite tense in accordance with the number and gender of the nominative. For example:

मैं खेला हूंगा main khela hoonga
I might have played   1st per. sin. mas.

99

मैं खेली हूंगी main kheli hoongi
I might have played   1st per. sing. fem.

हम खेले होंगे ham khele honge
we might have played   ,, plu. mas.

हम खेली हूंगी ham kheli hoongi
we might have played   ,, ,, fem.

तू खेला होगा tu khela hoga
you might have played   2nd sin. mas.

तुम खेले होगे tum khele hoge
you might had played   ,, plu. ,,

तू खेली होगी tu kheli hogi
you might have played   ,, sin. fem.

तुम खेली होगी tum kheli hogi
you might have played   ,, plu. ,,

वह खेला होगा woh khela hoga
he might have played   3rd sing. mas.

वे खेले होंगे way khele honge
they might have played   ,, plu. ,,

वह खेली होगी woh kheli hogi
she might have played   ,, sin. fem.

वे खेली हूंगी way kheli hoongi
they might have played   ,, plu. ,,

[V] Past Continuous (तात्कालिक भूतकाल) tatkalak bhoot)

This tense is formed by adding the past tense of the verb 'होना' to the Present Continuous tense. For example.

मैं खेल रहा था main khel raha tha
I was playing   1st person sin. mas.

मैं खेल रही थी main khel
rahi thi = I was playing   ,,   sin. fem.

हम खेल रहे थे ham khel
rahe thay = we were playing ,,   plu. mas.

हम खेल रही थीं ham khel
rahi theen = we were playing ,,   ,,   fem.

तू खेल रहा था tu khel raha tha
you were playing   2nd   ,,   sin. mas.

तुम खेल रहे थे tum khel
rahe they = you were playing ,,   plu. ,,

तू खेल रही थी tu khel rahi thee
you were playing   ,,   sin. fem.

तुम खेल रही थीं tum khel rahi
theen = you were playing   ,,   plu. ,,

वह खेल रहा था woh khel raha
tha = he was playing   3rd   ,,   sin. mas.

वे खेल रहे थे way khel rahe
thay = they were playing   ,,   plu. ,,

वह खेल रही थी woh khel rahi thi = she was playing   3rd per. sin. fem.

वे खेल रही थीं way khel rahi theen = they were playing   ,,   plu   ,,

VI Past Conditional हेतु हेतु मद भूत
haitu haitu mad bhoot

In this tense the past action is shown as dependent on some other action in the past.

Examples

मैं जाता यदि वह आया होता
main jata yadi woh aaya hota
If he had come I would heve gone

यदि वह मेहनत करता तो पास हो जाता
yadi woh mehnat karta to pass ho jata
If he had worked hard he would have passed

मैं खेलता यदि तू आता
main khelta yadi tu aata
If you had come I would have played

Future Tense
(भविष्यत् काल)

Mainly there is only one kind of future tense in Hindi and that is commonly known

as Future Indefinite Tense (भविष्यत्काल)

Examples

मैं खाऊँगा   main khaonga = I will eat
   1st per. sin. mas.

मैं खाऊँगी   main khaongi = I will eat
   1st per. sin. fem.

हम खाएंगे   ham khaenge = we will eat
   1st per. plu. mas.

हम खाएंगी   ham khaengi = we will eat
   1st per. plu. fem.

तू खाएगा   tu khaega = you will eat
   2nd per. sin. mas.

तू खाएगी   tu khaegi = you will eat
   2nd per. sin. fem.

तुम खाओगे   tum khaoge = you will eat
   2nd per. sin. mas.

तुम खाओगी   tum khaogi = you will eat
   2nd per plu. fem.

वह खाएगा   woh khaega = he will eat
   3rd per. sin. mas.

वह खाएगी   woh khaegi = she will eat
   3rd per. sin. fem.

वे खाएंगे   way khaenge = they will eat
   3rd per. plu. mas.

103

वे खाएंगी way khaengi = they will eat
3rd per. plu. fem.

Future Doubtful सम्भाव्य भविष्यत्
sambhaviya bhavishat

In this tense, the possibility of something happening in the future is indicated.

Examples

शायद आज मेरा मित्र आये
shayad, aaj mera mitr aaye
perhaps my friend comes today
OR
my friend may come today

This is regarding the use of third person मित्र (friend)

1st person

शायद मैं आज तेरे घर आऊँ
shayad main aaj tere ghar aaon
perhaps I come to your house today
OR
I may come to your house today

2nd person

शायद तू बहां जाए
shayad tu wahan jaye
perhaps you go there
OR
you may go there

In the above three examples we have seen that this tense is formed by adding to the root verb जा (go), आ (come) ये in the third person, ऊँ in the first person and ए in the second person.

Exercises

Translate into Hindi and indicate the related tense :

(1) I take tea (2) we go to school
(3) he goes to market
(4) she eats bread (5) I will read a book
(6) you will take milk
(7) he will come there in the night
(8) we will be in Agra tomorrow
(9) we will go there.
(10) what will you do tomorrow?
(11) they will meet me in the evening
(12) I was in Delhi yesterday
(13) sarla was thirsty
(14) when did you go to the town ?
(15) the boy ate the fruit
(16) the girls ate bread
(17) he has come here
(18) he has gone to Calcutta
(19) we are going
(20) we were going there

Ans.

(१) मैं चाय पीता हूं (present)
(२) हम स्कूल जाते हैं (present)
(३) वह मार्केट (बाजार) जाता है (present)
(४) वह रोटी खाती है (present)
(५) मैं पुस्तक पढ़ूंगा (future)
(६) तुम दूध पियोगे (future)
(७) वह रात में वहां आयेगा (future)
(८) हम कल आगरा में होंगे (future)
(९) हम वहाँ जाएँगे (future)
(१०) तुम कल क्या करोगे (future)
(११) वे मुझे सांयंकाल को मिलेंगे (future)
(१२) मैं कल दिल्ली में था (past)
(१३) सरला प्यासी थी (past)
(१४) तुम शहर कब गये थे (past)
(१५) लड़के ने फल खाया (past)
(१६) लड़कियों ने रोटी खाई (past)
(१७) वह यहाँ आया है (present perfect)
(१८) वह कलकत्ता गया है (present perfect)
(१९) हम जा रहे हैं (present continuous)
(२०) हम वहाँ जा रहे थे (past continuous)

Habitnal past tense
(अभ्यास बोधक भूत काल)

This tense is employed when some habit is to be expressed. For instance if we have to say **I used to read**, its translation in Hindi will be as follows :

मैं पढ़ा करता था (main parha karta tha)
                    1st person singular mas.

मैं पढ़ा करती थी (main parha karti thi)
                    1st person sin. fem.
(I used to read)

तू पढ़ा करता था (tu parha karta tha)
                    2nd person sin. mas.

तू पढ़ा करती थी (tu parha karti thi)
                    2nd person sin. fem.
(you used to read)

वह पढ़ा करता था (woh parha karta tha)
                    3rd person sin. mas.

वह पढ़ा करती थी (woh parha karti thi)
                    3rd person sin. fem.
(he/she used to read)

हम पढ़ा करते थे (ham parha karte thay)
                    1st person plu. mas.

हम पढ़ा करती थीं (ham parha karti theen)
                    1st person plu. fem.
(we used to read)

तुम पढ़ा करते थे (tum parha karte they)
                    2nd person plu. mas.

तुम पढ़ा करती थीं (tum parha karti theen)
2nd person plu. fem.
(you used to read)

वे पढ़ा करते थे way parha karte thay
3rd person plu. mas.

वे पढ़ा करती थीं way parha karti theen
3rd person plu. fem.
(they used to read)

Similarly habitual present and future can be formed.

Exercises

Translate into Hindi

(1) I used to go there in the night (2) We used to go to hospital (3) I used to bathe every day (4) We used to eat meat (5) They will be eating

Ans.

(1) मैं वहां रात को जाया करता था
(2) हम अस्पताल जाया करते थे
(3) मैं प्रतिदिन नहाया करता था
(4) हम मांस खाया करते थे
(5) वे खाते रहेंगे

108

LESSON 13
AUXILIARY VERBS

(सहायक क्रियाए)

There are certain verbs which supplement the main verbs in the sentence. They are called auxiliary verbs. Sometimes the auxiliary verbs are used as the main verbs.

The auxiliary verbs are—सक (can could), लग (do), चाह (want), दे (let do), चुक (do), पा (could).

सक—मैं जा सकता हूँ (main ja sakta hun = I can go). In this sentence the main verb 'go' is supplemented by सक (can)

मैं जा सकना था main ja sakta tha
I could go

तुम जा सकते थे tum ja sakte thay
You could go

वह जा सकता था woh ja sakta tha
he could go

वह जा सकती थी woh ja sakti thi
she could go

लग—वह चलने लगा (Woh chalne laga = He began to walk) In this sentence the main

verb 'walk' is supplemented by the auxiliary
लगा—चलने लगा (began to walk)

तुम चलने लगे tum chalne lage
you began to walk

वह चलने लगा woh chalne laga
he began to walk

वह चलने लगी woh chalne lagi
she began to walk

चाह—मैं सोना चाहता हू main sona chahta hun (I want to sleep). In this sentence the main verb 'सोना' is supplemented by 'चहाता'

तुम सोना चाहते हो tum sona chahte ho
you want to sleep

वह सोना चाहता हैं woh sona chahta hai
he wants to sleep

वह सोना चाहती है woh sona chahti hai
she wants to sleep

वह सोना चाहते हैं woh sona chahte hain
they want to sleep

दे मुझे आने दो (mujhe ane do = let me come) In this sentence the main word आने (come) is supplemented by the auxiliary दो (let)

उसे जाने दो usse jane do
let him / her go

110

चुक—गाड़ी आ चुकी है (gari aa chuki hai = train has come)—In this sentence the main verb is 'आ' [come] which is completed with the help of the auxiliary 'चुक', changed into 'चुकी' in feminine in accordance with the gender of the subject.

Other examples :

मैं खाना खा चुका था
main khana kha chuka tha
I had taken my meals

वह परीक्षा पास कर चुका है
woh parikshya pass kar chuka hai
he has passed the examination

पा—

मैं वहां नहीं पहुंच पाया
main vahan naheen pahunch paya
I could not reach there

उसने यह पर्स पाया है
uss ne yeh purse paya hai
he has got this purse

Exercises

Translate into Hindi :—

(1) I can ride the horse
(2) You could not go to bazaar

(3) How did you hurt your finger?
(4) I wanted to go there early in the morning
(5) Let him take a rest for a while
(6) We have got these books from the school
(7) You have finished the book.

Ans :

(१) मैं घोड़े पर चढ़ सकता हूं
(२) तुम बाजार नहीं जा सके
(३) तुम्हारी अंगुली में चोट कैसे लगी
(४) मैं वहां प्रातःकाल ही जाना चाहता था
(५) उसे थोड़ी देर आराम कर लेने दो
(६) हमने यह पुस्तकें स्कूल से पाई हैं
(७) तुमने पुस्तक पढ़ ली है

LESSON 14

Compound Verbs

(संयुक्त क्रियाएँ)

Sometimes words are employed to stress a particular meaning When such duplication occurs in the case of verbs, the two verbs together are called compound verbs. Even in such cases the root of the main verb remains unchanged and the other verb joined to it. Both verbs conjugated together intensify the meaning.

The conjuncts are उठ (utth), पड़ (par), ले (lay), डाल (daal), जा (ja), रख (rakh) etc., etc.

Examples :—

उठ —आवाज़ सुनते ही मैं जाग उठा (awaz sunte hi main jag uttha = on hearing the sound I woke up). In this sentence the verb जागना (wake up) has been strengthened by the addition of the second verb उठा

खुशी के मारे वह नाच उठा (khushi ke mare woh nach uttha = out of joy he danced)

पड़—मुझे खाना खाना पड़ा (mujhe khana khana

para=I had to eat). In this sentence there is a compulsion.

There is another meaning of पड़ा— वह ठोकर खाकर गिर पड़ा (woh thokar khakar gir para=he stumbled and fell)

ले—यह कमीज शीघ्र ही बदल ले (yeh kameez sheeghar hi badal le=change into this shirt quickly)

स्कूल से आज छुट्टी ले ले—(skool se aaj chuti le le =take holiday away from school)

डाल—मैंने यह पुस्तक एक दिन में ही पढ़ डाली (main ne yeh pustak ek din main he parh dali=I read through this book in one day)

जल्दी से यह पुस्तक पढ़ डाल (jaldi se yeh pustak parh dal=read up this book quickly)

उसने एक दिन में सारी पुस्तक पढ़ डाली (uss ne ek din main sari pustak parh dali=he read up the whole book in one day)

जा—कर्ज़ लेकर भूल जाना आसान नहीं (karz le kar bhool jana aasan naheen=it is not easy to forget debt repayment)

वह कल वापिस चला जाएगा (woh kal vapis chala jayega=he will go back tomorrow)

रख—याद रखो बिना मेहनत कभी सफलता नहीं मिलती (yad rakho, bina mehnat kabhi safalta nahin milti = keep it in mind, no success without hard work)

उसने सारी तैयारी पहले ही कर रखी थी (us ne sari tayari pehle hi kar rakhi thi = he had made preparation before hand.)

LESSON 15

Participles

(कृदन्त)

In English ceratin adjectives are derived from verbs. They are called persent participles or past participles. In Hindi, there are three kinds of participles—present participle, past participle and conjunctive participle.

The present participle means addition of ता (masculine), ती (feminine) and ते (plural) to the root of the main verb. For example

खाते, खाती, खाता (**eating**)

Its use is made to qualify a noun or pronoun as if it were to work as adjective. For example

बोलता हुआ मनुष्य नीचे गिर पड़ा
bolta hua manushy gir para
(the man fell while talking).

बोलती हुई लड़की गिर पड़ी or बोलते हुए वे आदमी गिर पड़े
The girl fell while speaking
or
those people fell while speaking

The present participle is used when the action is shown to be continuing as in the above examples or when action is shown to have been completed as for instance

हमारे घर पहुंचते वर्षा बन्द हो गई

hamare ghar pahunchte varsha band ho gayee

(the rain stopped as we reached home)

When the completion of action is to be shown as immediate, the present participle 'ते' takes an additional 'ही', for example

चोर को देखते ही मैं चिल्ला पडा

chor ko dekhte he main chilla para

(I cried out on seeing the thief)

Sometimes for greater effect the present participle is repeated as खाते खाते, जाते जाते etc

जाते जाते वह पांच रुपये दे गया

jate jate woh panch rupai de gaya

(he gave five rupees as he went away)

वह जाता जाता खा रहा था

woh jata jata kha rha tha

(he was eating while going)

Repetition of participle shows repetition of action. Sometimes instead of repeating two words, the expression used is खाता हुआ (khata hua), जाता हुआ (jata hua)

वह खाता हुआ जा रहा था, वह जाता हुआ खा रहा था।

Past participle

The past participle is formed by the addition of आ to the root of the other verb. This is also used as an adjective.

गिर + आ = गिरा, मर + आ = मरा

गिरी हुई वस्तु नहीं उठानी थी

giri hui vastu nahin utthani thee

(no picking up of the fallen thing)

मरा हुआ पक्षी वहां गिरा

mara hua pakhshi vahan gira

(the dead bird fell there)

When the action is shown as completed in the past "ए" in place of 'आ' is added to the root of the main verb.

तीन दिन हुए उसे मरे हुए

teen din hue usse mare hue

three days have passed since he died

Conjunctive participle

This is formed by the addition of कर, के, करके etc to the root of the main verb. For example

खा कर, खाके, खा करके

This participle is used to indicate an adverbial phrase and not as adjective as in the earlier two cases.

खाना खाकर (खाना खाके) मैं स्कूल चला गया
khana khakar (khake) main skool chala gayaa
(having taken my meals I went to school)

LESSON 16
Moods
(विधि)

There are two moods—subjunctive and imperative

Subjunctive mood This mood expreses a a purpose a wish, a condition or doubt. This mood is generally used in verbs in one of the clausse in a sentence, the verb in the other clause is to be in the indicative mood.

मैं तुम्हें अपनी पुस्तकें देता हूँ कि तुम परीक्षा पास कर सको

main tumhein apni pustkein deta, hun keh tum pariksha pass kar sako

(I give you my books so that you can pass examination). This sentence shows the purpose of giving the books

भगवान, तुम्हारा कल्याण करे (Bhagwan tumhara kalyan kare = May God bless you). This shows a wish.

यदि मैं दिल्ली आया तो उसे मिलूँगा (yadi main dili aya to usse milonga = If I came to Delhi I shall meet him.) This sentence shows a condition.

मुझ कुछ मिले या न, मैं यह काम अवश्य करूँगा (mujhe kuchh mile ya na, main yeh kam avashy karoonga = whether I get something or not, I must do this work). In this sentence the mood is that of doubt or supposition.

Imperative mood (आज्ञावाचक विधि) : This mood expresses wish, order or permission. The following is the form in which the verbs are employed to indicate this mood.

बैठ (sit)	= बैठो (singular),	बैठिये (plural)
उठ (rise)	= उठो (,,),	उठिये (,,)
पढ़ (read)	= पढ़ो (,,),	पढ़िये (,,)
आ (come)	= आओ (,,),	आइए (,,)
जा (go)	= जाओ (,,),	जाइए (,,)
ला (bring)	= लाओ (,,),	लाइए (,,)
खा (eat)	= खाओ (,,),	खाइए (,,)
दे (give)	= दो (,,),	दीजिए (,,)
कर (do)	= करो (,,),	करिए (,,)
देख (see)	= देखो (,,),	देखिए (,,)
भाग (run)	= भागो (,,),	भागिए (,,)

Singular—किताब पढ़ो (kitab parho = read the book). This shows an order

Plural — किताब पढ़िए (kitab parhiye = read the book)

Singular—मैं जाऊँ ? (main jaon = May I go) This shows permission

Plural — हम जाएँ (ham jayen = May we go ?)

Singular — तुम खाओ (tum khao = Please eat)
This shows wish

Plural — आप खाएँ (aap khayen = please eat)

Voice (वाच्य = vachya)

There are three kinds of voices in Hindi—active voice (कर्तृवाच्य). passive voice (कर्मवाच्य) and Intransitive passive (भाववच्या) or impersonal voice.

The function of the voice is to show whether in a particular sentence the subject or the object of a verb is prominent.

In the **Active voice** (कर्तृवाच्य) the importance is given to the subject. For example :

मैं पत्र लिखता हूं (main patr likhta hun = I write a letter). In this sentence मैं (subject) is important hence the stress on it. But if object is to be given prominence, the verb gets an additional 'जाना' in the past tense and the subject takes the case-ending से (with). Then it becomes **passive voice** :

मुझ से पत्र लिखा जाता है or पत्र मुझ से लिखा जाता है (mujh se patr likha jata hai = the letter is written by me)

In the Intransitive passive voice, the verb used is to be transitive and remains in the third person irrespective of the number and gender of the object or subject. In the third person its number is always singular and gender masculine.

मैं पढ़ नहीं सकता (active voice)

मुझ से पढ़ा नहीं जाता (Intransitive passive voice)

वे गए थे (active)

उनसे आया गया था (Intra. pass)

LESSON 17

Adverb

(क्रियाविशेषण)

Words which denote some particular aspect of the verb in a sentence are called adverb. For example 'walk slowly'. In this sentence the action of walking has been modified by the addition of the verb 'slowly', therefore 'slowly' is adverb. Sometimes even the verb is qualified by the addition of another modifying word such as 'walk too slowly' 'बहुत धीरे चलो'. Such words are also called adverbs.

Depending on the meaning, the adverbs are of four kinds :

Adverb of time (कालवाचक क्रियाविशेषण)

This type of adverb expresses time e.g. जब (when), कब (when), श्राज (today), कल (yesterday), प्रतिदिन (daily), पहले (before), पीछे (after), शीघ्र (quickly), प्रातः (morning), सायं (evening), रात (night) प्रायः (often), फिर (again), सदा (always) हरदिन (every day), कभी कभी (ever) कभी कभी (sometimes) etc. etc.

Adverb of place (स्थानवाचक क्रियाविशेषण)

Words which modify the meaning of the place of action are called adverb of place e.g. निकट (near), दूर (far off), यहाँ (here), वहाँ (there), ऊपर (above), नीचे (down), दायें (right), बायें (left), इस तरफ (this side), उस तरफ (that side), किधर (where), अन्दर (inside), बाहर (outside), आसपास (near about), चारों ओर (on all sides), सब जगह (everywhere) etc etc.

Adverb of quantity (परिमाणवाचक क्रियाविशेषण)

Words which modify the meaning of the quality of the verb are called adverbs of quantity, e.g. बहुत (much), थोड़ा (a little), बहुत थोड़ा (very little), कुछ (some), जरा (a little), पर्याप्त (enough), अधिक (more), केवल (only), बारी बारी से (in turn) बिल्कुल (entire), लगभग (nearly), खूब (very much) etc etc.

Adverb of manners (रीतिवाचक क्रियाविशेषण)

Words which denote the manner of doing action (verb) are called adverbs of manners e.g. धीरे धीरे (slowly), अचानक (suddenly), एकाएक (all of a sudden), शान्ति से (peacefully), हंसता हुआ (laughing), झटपट

(quickly), ध्यानपूर्वक (carefully) etc.

The adverbs of manners are not much in numbers.

Adverb of negation and affirmation

(निषेधवाचक तथा स्वीकृतिवाचक क्रियाविशेषण)

These adverbs express 'no' or 'yes' of the verbs such as नहीं (no), मत (don't) तनिक भी नहीं (not at all), निःसन्देह (without doubt), हाँ (yes), अवश्य (must), वास्तव में (in reality) etc.

Exercises

Distinguish the type of adverb and the adverb also in the following sentences :

१ दिन-रात खूब मेहनत करो

२ लगातार मेहनत का फल अच्छा होता है

३ सड़क पार करते समय इधर-उधर मत देखो

४ कुछ खा लो

५ धड़ाधड़ मत भागो नहीं तो अचानक गिर पड़ोगे

६ रेलगाड़ी २० मील की गति से चलती है

७ धीरे-धीरे उसकी गति तेज होती है
८ चलते-फिरते, खाते-पीते, उठते-बैठते भगवान का ध्यान रखो

Ans.

१ दिन-रात	(कालवाचक)
खूब	(परिमाणवाचक)
२ लगातार	(कालवाचक)
३ इधर-उधर	(स्थानवाचक)
५ कुछ	(परिमाणवाचक)
६ २०-मील	(परिमाणवाचक)
७ धीरे-धीरे	(रीतिवाचक)
८ खाते-पीते	,,
उठते-बैठते	,,

LESSON 18

Pronoun
(सर्वनाम)

A pronoun is a word which is used in place of a noun. The number and the gender of a pronoun are formed in accordance with those of the noun.

There are six types of pronoun :

(I) पुरुषवाचक सर्वनाम (**Purushvachak Sarvnam = Personal pronoun**). These pronouns are मैं (I), तू (you), वह (he)

Examples :

1st person :

मैं वहां जाता हूं main vahan jata hun
I go there   sin. mas.

मैं वहां जाती है main vahan jati hun
I go there   sin. fem.

हम (हम लोग) वहां जाते हैं
hum (humlog) vahan jate hain
we go there   plu. mas.

हम वहां जाती हैं ham vahan jati hain
we go there   plu. fem.

2nd person :

तू क्या करता है ? tu kiya karta hai
what do you do ?   sin. mas.

तू क्या करती है? tu kiya karti hai
what do you do? sin. fem.

तुम क्या करते हो? tum kiya karte ho
what do you do? plu. mas.

तुम क्या करती हो? tum kiya karti ho
what do you do? plu. fem.

3rd person :

वह क्या करता है? woh kiya karta hai
what does he do? sin. mas.

वह क्या करती है? woh kiya karti hai
what does she do? sin. fem.

वे क्या करते हैं? way kiya karte hain
what do they do? plu. mas.

वे क्या करती हैं? way kiya karti hain
what do they do? plu. fem.

(II) सम्बन्धवाचक सर्वनाम (sambandhvachak = Relative pronoun). In this category fall pronouns like जो and सो। Here the two pronouns used in one sentence connect each other. For example :

जो देता है सो लेता है
jo deta hai so leta hai
he who gives, takes

129

जिसकी लाठी उसकी भैंस
jiski lathi uski bhains
might is right

Other Examples—

जो सोता है सो खोता है
jo sota hai so khota hai
one who sleeps, loses

राम, जो मेरा भाई है, वह इस दफ्तर में काम करता है
Ram, jo mera bhai hai, woh iss daftar main kam karta hai
Ram, who is my brother, works in this office

(III) निजवाचक सर्वनाम (Nijvachak=Reflexive pronoun). Where for oneself the word 'आप', 'स्वयं' etc. is used, it is called निजवाचक सर्वनाम For example :

यह काम मैं आप ही कर लूंगा
yeh kam main aap hi kar loonga
I will myself do this work

यह काम वह स्वयं ही कर लेगा
yeh kam woh soyam hi kar lega
He will himself do this work

यह काम तुम आप (स्वयं) ही कर लोगे
yeh kam tum aap (soyam) hi kar loge
you will yourself do this work

(IV) प्रश्नवाचक सर्वनाम (prashanvachak = Interrogative pronoun). This pronoun expresses question in words like क्या (what), कौन (who)

Examples :

यह क्या है yeh kiya hai = what is this?
तुम क्या चाहते हो tum kiya chahte ho
what do you want?
वह कौन है woh kaun hai = who is he?
क्या पढ़ते हो kiya parhte ho
what do you read?
कौन काम करता है kaun kam karta hai
who works?

(V) संकेतवाचक सर्वनाम (Sanketvachak = Demonstrative pronoun). This pronoun gives expression to particular things, near or far e.g. यह (this), वह (that). This pronoun is also called निश्चयवाचक (nishchevachak) because it demonstrates a particular thing.

यह मेरी पुस्तक है yeh meri pustak hai
this is my book
ये मेरी पुस्तकें हैं ye meri pustkain hain
these are my books
वह आपकी कलम है woh aapki kalam hai
that is your pen
वे आपकी कलमें हैं way aapki kalmain hain
those are your pens

(VI) अनिश्चयवाचक सर्वनाम (Anishcheyvachak = Indefinite pronoun). This pronoun refers to expressions which do not give definite information about other things e.g. कोई (somebody) कुछ (something). In this category fall only these two pronouns.

कोई आया था koi aya tha
somebody had come

आपके लिए कुछ लाया था
aap ke liye kuchh laya tha
had brought something for you

LESSON 19

Adjective

(विशेषण)

Adjectives are words which qualify a noun or pronoun e.g. काला लड़का (kala larka = black boy). In this sentence काला is an adjective.

In English the adjective does not change its form with the change in the number or gender of the noun or pronoun it qualifies, but in Hindi it is a different story. The form of the adjective undergoes a change in accordance with the gender and number of the qualifying noun or pronoun. For example

काला लड़का (black boy)
काली लड़की (kali larki = black girl) sig. fem.
काले लड़के (kale larke = black boys) plu. mas.
काली लड़कियां (kali larkian-black girls)
    plu. fem.

As is clear from the above examples, the adjective changes its form in accordance with the number and gender of the masculine noun following it, but in the case of feminine noun singular or plural, the adjective retains the same form. In English we could have said :

'black boy', 'black girl', black boys' 'black girls' etc.

There are six types of Hindi adjectives:
1. गुणवाचक विशेषण (Adjective of quality)
2. परिमाणवाचक विशेषण (Adjective of quantity)
3. संख्यावाचक विशेषण (Numeral adjective)
4. सर्वनामिक विशेषण (Demonstrative adjective)
5. व्यक्तिवाचक विशेषण (Proper adjective)
6. प्रश्नवाचक विशेषण (Interrogative adjective)

1. गुणवाचक (gunvachak) : This adjective expresses qualities of a thing or a person

वीर आदमी (vir admi=brave man), डरपोक सैनिक (darpok sainik=coward soldier) काला कागज़ (kala kagaz=black paper), सुन्दर लड़की (sundar larki=beautiful girl), मासिक पत्र (masik patr=monthly), बंगाली मिठाई (Bangali mithai=Bengali sweatmeat)

other such adjectives are :

शूर (shoor=brave), दुर्बल (durbal=weak), पीला (peela=yellow), लाल (lal=red), सफेद (safed=white), नीला (neela=blue), भद्दा (bhada=ugly), देशी (deshi=native), विदेशी (videshi=foreign), प्रातःकालीन (pratakaleen=morning) सायंकालीन (sayankalin=evening), साप्ताहिक (saptahik=weekly), पाख्विक (pakhvik=fortnightly).

134

When it is to be indicated that the quality of a thing or person is in a little degree, we add the word 'सा' (sa) to the adjective e.g. काला सा फूल (kala sa phool=a little black flower), छोटा सा आदमी (chota sa admi=a small man) etc.

2. परिमाणवाचक (Parimanvachak): An adjective which qualifies a quantity or measure of a thing.

चार मीटर (char meter=four metres), थोड़ा पानी (thora pani=a little water), बहुत दूध (bahut doodh=much milk)

3. संख्यावाचक (sankhiyavachak):

This is an adjective which expresses the number of a person or thing. e.g. पहला घर (pahla ghar=first house), छटा कमरा (chhata kamra=sixth room), दूसरी गाय (doosri gayai= second cow).

4. सार्वनामिक (sarvnamik): Adjective made of such words as 'यह' (yeh=this), 'वह' (woh= that), 'इस' (iss=this), 'उस' (uss=that) are called सार्वनामिक or संकेतवाचक because these point to some particular person or thing.

Examples

यह बालक अच्छा है yeh balak achha hai
this boy is good

वह घोड़ा अच्छा है woh ghora achha hai
that horse is good

इस बन्दर ने फल तोड़ा iss bandar ne phal tora
this monkey plucked the fruit

उस गाय ने दूध दिया uss gayai ne doodh diya
that cow gave milk

5. **व्यक्तिवाचक (vayaktivachak)** : This adjective denotes some speciality of a person or thing Some authors include this in गुणवाचक सर्बनाम also e.g.

बंगाली मिठाई bangali mithai
Bengali sweets

पंजाबी गेहूँ punjabi geyhun — Punjabi wheat

पाकिस्तानी एक्टर Pakistani actor etc.

6. **प्रश्नवाचक (prashanvachak)** : This adjective refers to questions about a particular person or thing eg.

क्या नाम रखा है ? kiya nam rakha hai
what name has been given ?

कौन सा रंग अच्छा है ? kaunsa rang achha hai
which colour is good ?

Degree of Comparison
विशेषणों की तुलना

There are three degrees of comparison :

मूल:वस्था (positive degree) उत्तरावस्था (comparative degree) and उत्तमावस्था (superlative degree)

1. **मूलावस्था** (moolavastha) : This degree indicates general quality—राम समझदार है (Ram samaihdar hai = Ram is wise)

2. **उत्तरावस्था** (utaravastha) : This degree shows comparison between two persons or things—राम श्याम से अधिक समझदार है (Ram, Shyam se adhik samajdar hai = Ram is wiser than Shyam)

3. **उत्तमावस्था** (uttamavastha) : This degree indicates the best quality in man or thing e.g. राम सब लड़कों से अच्छा है (Ram sab larkoon se achha hai = Ram is the best boy)

So we can say—अच्छा, अधिक अच्छा, सबसे अच्छा in the three degrees. In denoting the degree of an adjective, the adjective itself does not undergo any change.

Some adjectives are used in pairs eg.

मैला-कुचैला कपड़ा   maila-kuchela kapra
very dirty cloth

साफ-सुथरा कमरा   saf-suthra kamra
very clean room

सड़ा-गला फल   sara-galla phal
very rotten fruit

Exercises

Correct the following :

१ काला लड़की २ दो-गज़ लम्बा दीवार
३ काला लड़के ४ थोड़ी पानी
५ छटी मकान
६ राम, कृष्ण से सब से अच्छा लड़का है
७ राम, कृष्ण से बुद्धिमान है
८ वह घोड़ा अच्छी है ९ क्या करनी है
१० कौन-सी फिल्म अच्छा है

Ans.

१ काली लड़की २ दौ-गज़ लम्बी दीवार
३ काले लड़के ४ थोड़ा पानी
५ छटा मकान
६ राम कृष्ण से अधिक अच्छा लड़का है
७ राम कृष्ण से अधिक बुद्धिमान है
८ वह घोड़ा अच्छा है ९ क्या करना है ?
१० कौन-सी फिल्म अच्छी है

Important adjectives
(आवश्यक क्रियाविशेषण)

Active = फुर्तीला, चुस्त phurteela, chust
Angry = क्रोधित, नाराज़ karodhit, naraaz
Bad = बुरा bura
Beautiful = सुन्दर sundar
Bitter = कड़वा karwa

Blind = अन्धा andha
Brave = बहादुर bahadur
Careful = सचेत sachet
Clean = साफ़ saaf
Clear = निर्मल nirmal
Clever = चालाक chalak
Cold = ठंडा thanda
Common = साधारण sadharan
Cruel = निर्दयी nirdaye
Deaf = बहरा bahra
Difficult = कठिन kathin
Dirty = मैला maila
Dishonest = बे-ईमान beiman
Dry = सूखा sookha
Dusty = धूल-भरा dhool bhara
Early = जल्दी jaldi
Easy = आसान aasan
Empty = खाली khali
Equal = समान saman
False = झूठा jhoota
Famous = प्रसिद्ध prasidh
Fat = मोटा mota
Favourable = अनुकूल anukul
Fine = उत्तम uttam
Foolish = मूर्ख murakh
Fortunate = भाग्यवान bhagyavan

Fresh = ताज़ा taza
Gay = खुश khush
Generous = उदार udar
Gentle = नेक nek
Good = अच्छा achha
Great = बड़ा bara
Happy = खुश khush
Hard = कठोर kathor
Healthy = स्वस्थ swasth
Heavy = भारी bhari
High = ऊंचा uncha
Hollow = पोला pola
Hot = गरम garam
hungry = भूखा bhookha
Important = आवश्यक avashyak
Innocent = निर्दोष nirdosh
Lame = लंगड़ा langra
Large = बड़ा bara
Lazy = आलसी alsi
Lean = दुबला dubla
Light = हलका halka
Long = लम्बा lamba
Loose = ढीला dheela
Loud = ऊंचा uncha
Lucky = भाग्यवान bhagyvan
Mad = पागल pagal

Modern = आधुनिक aadhunik
Muddy = गदला gandla
Naked = नंगा nanga
Necessary = आवश्यक aavashyak
New = नया naya
Noble = कुलीन kuleen
Old = बूढ़ा boorha
Open = खुला khula
Pale = फीका pheeka
Perfect = पक्का pucca
Pleasant = सुहावना suhawna
Poisonous = विषैला vishaila
Polite = नम्र namr
Poor = गरीब garib
Present = वर्तमान vartman
Private = निजी niji
Proud = घमंडी ghamandi
Pure = शुद्ध shudh
Quiet = चुप chup
Rare = विरला virla
Raw = कच्चा kacha
Real = असली asli
Reliable = विश्वासयोग्य vishwasyogya
Rich = धनी dhani
Right = ठीक theek
Ripe = पका pucca

Round = गोल gol
Rural = देहाती dehati
Safe = सुरक्षित surakhit
Serious = गम्भीर gambhir
Severe = कड़ा kara
Sharp = तेज़ tez
Short = छोटा chhota
Silent = चुप chup
Simple = सादा sada
Single = अकेला akela
Slow = धीमा dheema
Small = छोटा chhota
Soft = नरम naram
Sour = खट्टा khatta
Stormy = तूफ़ानी toofani
Strange = विचित्र vichitar
Strong = बलवान balwan
Sure = निश्चित nishchit
Sweet = मीठा meetha
Tall = लम्बा lamba
Terrible = भयंकर bhayankar
Thick = मोटा mota
Thin = पतला patla
Thirsty = प्यासा piyasa
Tight = तंग tang
Tired = थका हुआ thaka hua

True = सच्चा sacha
Ugly = भद्दा bhada
Urgent = आवश्यक avashyak
Useful = लाभदायक labhdayak
Violent = हिंसुक hinsuk
Warm = गरम garam
Weak = कमजोर kamzor
Wet = भीगा bheega
Wicked = दुष्ट dusht
Willing = राजी razi
Wild = जंगली jangli
Wooden = लकड़ी का lakri ka
Young = ज्वान jawan

LESSON 20

Imperatives and useful expressions

Ask me मुझसे पूछो (mujh se poocho)
Ask him उससे पूछो (uss se poocho)
Ask them उनसे पूछो (unse poocho)
Bring an answer उत्तर लाओ (utar lao)
Bring my luggage मेरा सामान लाओ
 (mera saman lao)
Bring water पानी लाओ (pani lao)
Bring my clothes मेरे कपड़े लाओ
 (mere kapre lao)
Bring me some ice मेरे लिए कुछ बर्फ लाओ
 (mere liye kuchh baraf lao)
Bring some fruit कुछ फल लाओ (kuch phal lao)
Bring a cup एक प्याला लाओ (ek piyala lao)
Bring a clean vessel एक साफ बर्तन लाओ
 (ek saf bartan lao)
Boil some eggs कुछ अंडे उबालो
 (kuchh ande ubalo)
Burn this इसको जला दो (isko jala do)
Be careful सावधान (savdhan)
Be silent चुप रहो (chup raho)
Call him उसको बुलाओ (usko bulao)
Call them उन्हें बुलाओ (unhe bulao)

Call them here उन्हें यहाँ बुलाओ
 (unhein yahan bulao)

Call a taxi टैक्सी बुलाओ (teksi bulao)

Call the servant नौकर को बुलाओ
 (nokar ko bulao)

Call Mr. Ali अली साहिब को बुलाओ
 (ali sahib ko bulao)

Call a barber नाई को बुलाओ (nai ko bulao)

Come near पास आओ (pas ao)

Clean properly ठीक से साफ करो
 (theek se saf karo)

Change your clothes कपड़े बदलो (kapre badlo)

Come in time समय पर आओ (samay par ao)

Come later बाद में आना (bad mein ana)

Come to my house मेरे घर आओ (mere ghar ao)

Come back लौट आओ (laut ao)

Cook it इसे पकाओ (ise pakao)

Carry out my order मेरी आज्ञा मानो
 (meri agya mano)

Come near me मेरे निकट आओ
 (mere nikat ao)

Cut my hair मेरे बाल काटो (mere bal kato)

Clean the comb कंघी साफ करो
 (kanghi saf karo)

Count my clothes मेरे कपड़े गिनो
    (mere kapre gino)

Change this tyre इस टायर को बदलो
    (iss tayr ko badlo)

Drive me to hotel मुझे होटल ले चलो
    (mujhe hotal le chalo)

Go to the hotal होटल जाओ (hotal jao)

Go slowly धीरे धीरे जाओ (dheere dheere jao)

Go quickly तेज़ तेज़ जाओ (tez tez jao)

Go at once एक दम जाओ (ek dam jao)

Go straight सीधे जाओ (seedhe jao)

Go away चले जाओ (chale jao)

Go and bring my books जाओ और मेरी पुस्तकें लाओ
    (jao aur meri pustkein lao)

Go up ऊपर जाओ (upar jao)

Go down नीचे जाओ (neeche jao)

Go to bed सो जाओ (so jao)

Go to the market बाज़ार जाओ (bazar jao)

Give me मुझे दो (mujhe do)

Give me that book वह पुस्तक मुझे दो
    (woh pustak mujhe do)

Give him a chair उसे कुर्सी दो (usse kursi do)

Give my compliments मेरा प्रणाम कहना
    (mera parnam kehna)

Give me the key चाबी मुझे दो
(chabi mujhe do)
Get ready तैयार हो जाओ (tyar ho jao)
Get down उतर जाओ (utar jao)
Give me your number मुझे अपना नंबर दो
(mujhe apna namber do)
Get me water मुझे पानी दो (mujhe pani do)
Get up early सवेरे उठो (savere uttho)
Get out बाहर निकल जाओ (bahar nikal jao)
Good bye राम राम (Ram Ram)
Have a bath स्नान करो (sanan karo)
How far is it ? कितनी दूर है (kitni door hai)
How excellent ! क्या खूब ! (kya khub)
He is not at home वह घर में नहीं है
(woh ghar mein nahin hai)
How much is the fare ? क्या भाड़ा है
(kya bhara hai)
How far is the station ? स्टेशन कितनी दूर है
(sateshan kitni door hai)
Have you made the tea ? क्या तुमने चाय बना ली है
(kiya tumne chay banali hai)
He stumbles वह ठोकर खाता है
(woh thokar khata hai)
He died वह मर गया (woh mar gaya)

He has gone for a walk वह सैर को गया है
(woh sair ko gaya hai)

He will come back soon वह शीघ्र लौट आयेगा
(woh sheegar laot ayega)

Have you any relation ? तुम्हारे कोई भाई बंद हैं
(tumhare koi bhai band hai)

He is my elder brother वह मेरा बड़ा भाई है
How old are you ? तुम्हारी आयु क्या है
(tumhari ayu kya hai)

He worships one God वह एक भगवान की पूजा करता है
(woh ek bhagwan ki puja karta hai)

Look here इधर देखो (idhar dekho)
Listen सुनो (suno)
Leave it alone इसे रहने दो (isse rehno do)
Light the lamp बत्ती जलाओ (bati jalao)
Lay the table मेज़ लगाओ (mez lagao)
Let me know मुझे बताओ (mujhe batao)
Let me tell मुझे कहने दो (mujhe kehno do)
Let me look मुझे देखने दो (mujhe dekhne do)
Leave the car here गाड़ी यहाँ छोड़ो
(gari yahan chhoro)

Make haste जल्दी करो (jaldi karo)
Make tea चाय बनाओ (chaye banao)
Make it easy आराम से बैठो (araam se baitho)
Make the bed बिस्तर लगाओ (bistar lagao)

My writing is not good मेरा लिखना साफ नहीं है
   (mera likhna saf nahin hai)
Oil the machine मशीन को तेल दो
   (masheen ko tal do)
Open the door दरवाजा खोलो (darwaza kholo)
Order a taxi टैक्सी मगाओ (teksi mangao)
Order a dinner भोजन मंगाओ (bhojan mangao)
Pour water पानी डालो (pani dalo)
Put it there इसे वहां रखो (isse wahan rakho)
Put it here इसे यहां रखो (isse yahan rakho)
Put my clothes in the car मेरे कपड़े गाड़ी में रखो
   (mere kapre gari main rakho)
Put ice into the glass ग्लास में बर्फ डालो
   (glas mein baraf dalo)
Put out the lamp बती बुझाओ (bati bujhao)
Put out the fire आग बुझाओ (aag bujhao)
Place it on the table इसे मेज पर रखो
   (isse mez par rakho)
Put down the luggage सामान नीचे रखो
   (saman neeche rakho)
Ring the bell घंटी बजाओ (ghanti bajao)
Remain quiet चुप रहो (chup raho)
Stop रुको (ruko)
Speak बोलो (bolo)
Sit down बैठ जाओ (baith jao)

149

Stand up खड़े हो जाओ (khare ho jao)
Shut up बकवास बन्द करो (bakwas band karo)
Shut the door दरवाजा बन्द करो
  (darwaza band karo)
Send for the coolie कुली को बुला भेजो
  (kuli ko bula bhejo)
Show me the menu मुझे मीनू दिखाओ
  (mujhe menu dikhao)
Show me the tariff मुझे निरखनामा दिखाओ
  (mujhe nirkhnama dikhao)
Show me a sample मुझे नमूना दिखाओ
  (mujhe namoona dikhao)
Show better quality अच्छी चीज दिखाओ
  (achhi cheez dikhao)
Stand still चुप खड़े रहो (chup khare raho)
Shave me very close बराबर हजामत करो
  (brabar hajamet karo)
Sweep the floor फर्श साफ़ करो (farash saf karo)
Sweep the carpet गालीचा झाड़ो (galeecha jharo)
Send him here उसे यहां भेजो (usse yahan bhejo)
Sign the cheque चेक पर हस्ताक्षर करो
  (check par hastakhar karo)
Show me the tonque मुझे जीभ दिखाओ
  (mujhe jibh dikhao)

Shut your eye अपनी आंखें बन्द करो
(apni ankhen band karo)
Turn to the left बायें मुड़ो (bayen murro)
Turn to the right दायें मुड़ो (dayen murro)
Turn back पीछे मुड़ो (peeche murro)
Take this यह लो (yeh lo)
Turn him out उसे बाहर निकालो
(usse baher nikalo)
This way इधर (idhar)
That way उधर (udhar)
Tell him to go away उसे कहो चला जाए
(usse kaho chale jaye)

That is too costly वह बहुत कीमती है
(woh bahut keemti hai)
Too soon बहुत जल्दी (bahut jaldi)
Toast the bread रोटी सेंको (roti sainko)
The egg is too hard अंडा बहुत कड़ा है
(anda bahut kara hai)
That will do बस (bus)
This room is dirty यह कमरा गंदा है
(yeh kamra ganda hai)
This shirt is dirty यह कमीज मैली है
(yeh kameez maili hai)
Take off your boots अपने जूते उतारो
(apne joote utaro)

151

Trim the moustache मूंछ छोटी कर दो
  (moonch chhoti kar do)
Take care of it उसको संभालो (usko sambhalo)
Take your seat कुर्सी पर बैठो (kursi par baitho)
Take something else कुछ और ले लो
  (kuchh aur lelo)
Wait outside बाहर ठहरो (bahar thero)
What a pity ! अफसोस (afsos)
What a shame ! लज्जा की बात है
  (lajja ki bat hai)
Which way किस ओर (kis aur)
What is the time ? कितना बजा है
  (kitana baja hai)
Whither ? किधर (kidhar)
Write his address उसका पता लिखो
  (uska pata likho)
Wait for an answer उत्तर की प्रतिक्षा करो
  (utar ki prateekhya karo)

LESSON 21

Use of 'No'

('न' का प्रयोग)

It is no matter कुछ नहीं (Kuchh nahin)

Don't trouble me मुझे तंग मत करो
(mujhe tang mat karo)

Do not come न आओ (na ao)

Do not forget मत भूलो (mat bhoolo)

Don't go without me मेरे विना मत जाओ
(mere vina mat jao)

Don't make a noise शोर मत करो (shor mat karo)

Don't bother me मुझे परेशान न करो
(mujhe pareshan na karo)

Don't ask me मुझसे मत पूछो (mujhe mat pucho)

Don't tell me मुझे मत बताओ (mujhse mat batao)

Don't fight मत लड़ो (mat laro)

No, Madame नहीं श्रीमती जी (nahin shrimatiji)

He is not at home वह घर में नहीं है
(woh ghar mein nahin hai)

Don't trouble yourself आप कष्ट न करें
(ap kasht na karein)

Don't beat the dog कुत्ते को मत मारो
(kute ko mat maro)

I do not know मुझे मालूम नहीं
    (mujhe maloom nahin)

Never tell a lie कभी झूठ न बोलो
    (kabhi jhoot na bolo)

Never steal कभी चोरी मत करो
    (kabhi chori mat karo)

Don't whip it इसे चाबुक न मारो
    (ise chabuk na maro)

I have no bedding मेरे पास बिस्तर नहीं है
    (mere pas bistar nahin hai)

I have no cash मेरे पास नकदी नहीं है
    (mere pas nakdi nahin hai)

Do not fire गोली मत चलाओ (goli mat chalao)

I have no appetite मुझे भूख नहीं
    (mujhe bhook nahin)

Do not wipe feet अपने पैर न पोंछो
    (apne paer na poncho)

No entrance अन्दर आने का रास्ता नहीं
    (andar ane ka rasta nahin)

No exit बाहर जाने का रास्ता नहीं
    (bahar jane ka rasta nahin)

No smoking धूम्रपान मना है
    (dhoomarpan manah hai)

Not very well बहुत अच्छा नहीं (bahut achha nahin)

I do not know मुझे मालूम नहीं
    (mujhe maloom nahin)

It is not allowed इसकी आज्ञा नहीं (iski agya nahin)

I do not like it मुझे यह पसन्द नहीं
    (mujhe yeh pasand nahin)

I do not want it मुझे यह नहीं चाहिए
    (mujhe yeh nahin chahiye)

Do not blame me मुझे दोष न दो
    (mujhe dosh na do)

It is not my fault यह मेरा दोष नहीं
    (yeh mera dosh nahin)

LESSON 22
Interrogations
(प्रश्नसूचक)

Is this my book ? क्या यह पुस्तक मेरी है ?
(kya yeh pustak meri hai)

Is he your brother ? क्या वह तुम्हारा भाई है
(kya woh tumhara bhai hai)

Is that your house ? क्या वह तुम्हारा घर है
(kya woh tumhara ghar hai)

Is this their home ? क्या यह उनका घर है
(kya yeh unka ghar hei)

Is the road good or bad ? क्या सड़क ठीक है अथवा खराब (kya sarak theek hai athwa kharab)

Is anyone there ? कोई है (koi hai) or वहाँ कोई है
(wahan koi hai)

Is he in ? क्या वह घर में हैं
(kya woh ghar men hain)

Is there any room ? जगह है (jagah hai)

Is this the last train ? क्या यह अन्तिम गाड़ी है
(kya yeh antim gari hai)

Is the colour fast ? क्या यह रंग पक्का है ?
(kya yeh rang paka hai)

Is this worth ten rupees ? क्या यह दस रुपये का माल है
(kya yeh das rupaye ka mal hai)

Is this letter for the post ? क्या यह पत्र डाक में डालना है ? kya yeh patr dak men dalna hai)

How are you ? आप कैसे हैं ? (ap kaise hain)

How do you do ? क्या हाल है (kya hal hai)

How much money ? कितना पैसा (kitna paisa)

How far is it ? कितनी दूर है (kitni door hai)

How excellent ? क्या खूब (kha khoob)

How much fare ? क्या भाड़ा ? (kya bhara)

How much have I to pay ? मुझे कितना पैसा देना है ? (mujhe kitna paisa dena hai)

How long does it stop ? यह कितनी देर यहां रुकती है ? (yeh kitni der yahan rookti hai)

How much is wanting ? कितना पैसा कम है ? (kitna paisa kam hai)

How much is the rent ? किराया क्या है ? (kiraya kya hai)

How many times a day ? दिन में कितनी बार ? (din main kitni bar,

How much duty must I pay ? मुझे कितना महसूल देना है ? (mujhe kitna mahsul dena hai)

How long you have been ill ? आप कब से बीमार हैं ? (ap kab se bimar hain)

What is your name ? तुम्हारा (आपका) क्या नाम है ? (tumhara—apka kya nam hai)

What is it ? यह क्या है ? (yeh kya hai)
What is the news ? क्या खबर है ?
(kya khabar hai)
What is to be done ? क्या किया जाए ?
(kya kiya jai)
What is that good for ? वह किस काम का ?
(who kis kam ka)
What is there for dinner ? खाने के वास्ते क्या है ?
(khane ke waste kya hai)
What is the time ? कितना बजा है ?
(kitna baja hai)
What is the matter ? क्या बात है ? (kya bat hai)
What do you want ? तुम्हें क्या चाहिए ?
(tumhe kya chahiye)
What does this mean ? इसका मतलब क्या है ?
(iska matlab kya hai)
what are your terms per day ?
दिन भर का भाड़ा क्या है ?
(din bhar ka bhara kya hai)
what is the price ?
कीमत क्या है ? (keemat kya hai)
what is the lowest price ? कम-से-कम कीमत क्या है ?
(kam-se-kam kimat kya hai)

what is the matter with you ?

तुम्हें क्या हुआ है ? (tumhein kya hua hai)

what is this thing ?

यह चीज क्या है ? (yeh cheez kya hai)

where is your office ?

तुम्हारा दफतर कहां है ?
(Tumhara daftar kahan hai)

where are you going ?

तुम कहां जा रहे हो ?
(tum kahan ja rahe ho)

where does he live ?

वह कहां रहता है ? (woh kahan rahta hai)

where can I get it ?

मुझे यह कहां मिल सकता है ?
(mujhe yeh kahan mil sakta hai)

where can I stay ?

मैं कहां ठहर सकता हूं ?
(main kahan thahr sakta hun)

where is the babe ?

बच्चा कहां है ? (bacha kahan hai)

where is your father ?

तुम्हारे पिता कहां हैं ?
(tumhare pita kahan hain)

Which is the nearest shop ?

सबसे अधिक नजदीक कौन सी दुकान है

(sabse adhik nazdeek kaunsi dookan hai)

which is the road to the hotel ?

होटल को कौनसी सड़क जाती है ?

(hotal ko kounsi sarak jati hai)

which is the train for Bombay ?

बम्बई की गाड़ी कौन सी है

(bambai ki gari kaunsi hai)

which is the biggest city ?

कौनसा शहर सबसे बड़ा है ?

(kaunsa shahr sabse bara hai)

When will you meet me ?

तुम मुझे कब मिलोगे ?

(tum mujhe kab miloge)

when will breakfast be ready ?

नाशता कब तैयार मिलेगा ?

(nashta kab tyar milega)

when do you start ?

तुम कब चल पड़ोगे ? (tum kab chal paroge)

when does the next train start ?

अगली गाड़ी कब छुटेगी ?

(agli gari kab chhutegi)

Why are you going ?

तुम क्यों जा रहे हो ? (tum kyun ja rahe ho)

why can't you come here ?

तुम यहां क्यों नहीं आ सकते ?
(tum yahan kiyun nahin a sakte)

Can you repair it ? क्या तुम इसे ठीक कर सकते हो ?
(kya tum ise theek kar sakte ho)

can I break journey ? क्या मैं यात्रा भंग कर सकता हूं ?
(kya mein yatra bhang kar sakta hun)

can I get refreshments? क्या मुझे यहां चाय पानी मिलेगा?
(kya mujhe yahan chay-pani milega)

can you cook ? क्या तुम खाना बना सकते हो ?
(kya tum khana bana sakte ho)

can you see me ? क्या तुम मुझे मिल सकते हो ?
(kya tum mujhe mil sakte ho)

can you pay in advance ?

क्या कुछ पेशगी दे सकते हो ?
(kya kuchh peshgi de sakte ho)

can you lend me this book ?

क्या तुम यह पुस्तक मुझे उधार दे सकते हो ?
(kya tum yeh pustak mujhe udhar de sakte ho)

LESSON 23

Some more expressions
(कुछ अधिक वाक्य)

In this chapter we will include those expressions which are used on particular occasions only. This is meant to widen the reader's knowledge of the spoken language.

About the shop (दुकान के विषय में)

Whose shop is this ?

यह दुकान किसकी है ? (yeh dukan kiski hai)

where is the shopkeeper ?

दुकानदार कहां है ? (dokandar kahan hai)

what is the price of this ?

इसका मूल्य क्या है ? (iska mulya kiya hai)

this is very dear

यह बहुत महंगा है (yeh bahut mehnga hai)

how much for a rupee ?

एक रुपया का कितना ? (ek rupaya ka kitna)

fifty paise per kg.

पच्चास पैसे प्रति किलो (pachas paise prati kilo)

what is the rate of wheat ?

गेहूं का क्या भाव है ? (gehun ka kya bhav hai)

162

forty rupees a quintal
　　चालीस रुपये प्रति क्विंटल
　　　(chalis rupaye parati kwintal)
show me some sample
　　मुझे कुछ नमूना दिखाओ
　　　(mujhe kuchh namoona dikhao)
have you got shirting ?
　　क्या तुम्हारे पास कमीजों का कपड़ा है
　　　(kya tumahre pas kameezoon ka kapra hai)
how much for a metre ?
　　एक मीटर का कितना (ek metar ka kitna)
two rupees fifty paise per metre
　　दो रुपये पच्चास पैसे प्रति मीटर
　　　(do rupaya pachas paise prati metar)
what is the length ?
　　इसकी लम्बाई क्या है ? (iski lambai kya hai)
give me the bill
　　इसका बिल (पर्चा) बनाओ
　　　(iska bil (parcha) banao)
I am grateful fo you मैं आपका अभारी हूं
　　　(mein apka abhari hun)

LESSON 24

Season and Weather (मौसम)

It is spring बसन्त है (vasant hai)

It is summer ग्रीष्म है (grishm hai)

It is rainy season वर्षा ऋतु है (varsha ritu hai)

It is autum पतझड़ है (patjhar hai)

It is winter जाड़ा है (jara hai)

It is cold today आज सर्दी है
  (aj sardi hai)

I am shivering मुझे कंपकंपी लगी है
  (mujhe kapkapi lagi hai)

It is hot today आज गर्मी है (as garmi hai)

I am perspiring मुझे पसीना आ रहा है
  (mujhe pasina a raha hai)

It is raining वर्षा हो रही है (varsha ho rahi hai)

I was drenched मैं भीग गया (mein bheeg gaya)

what a strong wind हवा कितनी तेज है
  (hawa kitni tej hai)

The weather is changing मौसम बदल रहा है
  (mausam badal raha hai)

The sky is cloudy आकाश में बादल है
  (akash mein badal hai)

The sun is not visible सूर्य दिखाई नहीं दे रहा है
    (sury dikhai nahin de raha hai)
It is getting cold सर्दी हो रही है
    (sardi ho rahi hai)
It is a bright night रात्रि में चांद निकला है
    (ratri mein chand nikla hai)
It is a full moon आज पूरा चांद निकला है
    (aj poora chand nikla hai)
The night is dark रात अन्धेरी है
    (rat andheri hai)
It has been snowing बर्फ़ पड़ रही है
    (baraf par rahi hai)

LESSON 25
Time
समय

Look at the watch घड़ी पर देखो (ghari par dekho)

what is the time now क्या बजा है (kya baja hai)

It is four o' clock चार बजे हैं (char baje hain)

It is quarter past four सवा चार बजे हैं
 (sawa char baje hain)

It is half past four साढ़े चार बजे हैं
 (sadhe char baje hain)

It is quarter to five पौने पांच बजे हैं
 (paone panch baje hain)

It is twenty minutes past four चार बज कर बीस मिनट हुए हैं (char bajkar bis mint hooye hain)

It is twenty minutes to four चार बजने में बीस मिनट हैं (char bajne mein bis mint hain)

It is ten a.m. दस बजे प्रातः (das baje pratah)

It is ten p.m. दस बजे रात (das baje rat)

It is 12 noon बारह बजे दोपहर (barh baje dopahr)

It is 12 midnight बारह बजे अर्ध रात
 (barah baje ardhrat)

My watch is fast मेरी घड़ी तेज है
 (meri ghari tej hai)

My watch is slow मेरी घड़ी पीछे है
 (meri ghari peechhe hai)
I am grateful to you मैं आपका आभारी हूं
 (mein apka abhari hun)
My watch has stopped मेरी घड़ी रुक गई है
 (meri ghari ruk gai hai)
My watch does not give correct time मेरी घड़ी ठीक समय नहीं देती (meri ghari thik samay nahin deti)
It has just struck eight घड़ी ने अभी आठ बजाए हैं
 (ghari ne abhi ath bajaye hain)
I am coming in half a minute मैं आधे मिनट में आ रहा हूं (mein adhe mint mein a raha hoon)
The train is 24 hours late गाड़ी २४ घंटे पीछे है
 (gari 24 ghante peeche hai)

LESSON 26

Requests and permission (प्रार्थना, मंज़ूरी)

May I come in please ? क्या मैं अन्दर आ सकता हूं ?
 (kya mein andar a sakta hoon)
Yes, with pleasure जी हां, खुशी से
 (jee, han khushi se)
You may come and go आप आ सकते हैं और जा सकते हैं (ap aa sakte hain aur ja sakte hain)
May I phone please ? क्या मैं फोन कर सकता हूं ?
 (kya main phon kar sakta hoon)
May I sit here ? क्या मैं यहां बैठ सकता हूं ?
 (kya main yahan baith sakta hoon)
Will you please give me a lift ? क्या आप मुझे अपने साथ गाड़ी में ले चलेंगे ? kya aap mujhe apne sath gari mein le chalenge)
Oh, yes, by all means हां, हां, बिल्कुल शौक से (han, han, bilkul shouk se)

LESSON 27

Apologies (क्षमा याचना)

I beg your pardon मैं आपसे क्षमा चाहता हूँ (main apse kshama chahta hoon)

Forgive me for not coming न आने के लिए क्षमा चाहता हूँ (na ane ke liye kshama chahta hoon)

Allow me to introduce myself मुझे अपना परिचय देने की आज्ञा दें (mujhe apna parichay dene ki agya den)

Please give my compliments to him कृपया उनसे मेरा नमस्कार कहिए (kripya unse mera namaskar kahiye)

So kind of you आपकी अति कृपा (apki ati kripa)

I am much obliged to you मैं आपका बहुत आभारी हूँ (main apka bahut abhari hoon)

Excuse me for this मुझे इसके लिए क्षमा करें (mujhe iske liye kshama karen)

Forgive me for coming late देरी के लिए क्षमा चाहता हूँ (deri ke liye kshama chahta hoon)

May I come in please ? क्या मैं अन्दर आ सकता हूँ (kya main andar aa sakta hoon)

Can I be of any service to you ? क्या मैं आपकी कोई सेवा कर सकता हूं ? (kya main apki koi sewa kar sakta hoon)

It doesn't matter कोई बात नहीं (koi bat nahin)

I am very sorry मुझे बहुत अफसोस है
(mujhe bahut afsos hai)

I am not at fault मेरा कोई दोष नहीं
(mera koi dosh nahin)

So sorry बहुत दु:ख हुआ (bahut dukh hua)

It was by mistake यह गलती हो गई
(yeh galti ho gai)

LESSON 28

Exercises for Reading
(पढ़ने का अभ्यास)

LETTERS

[I] For visit to a workshop

सेवा में

        श्री व्यवस्थापक महोदय,
        मार्डन बेंकरीज़, नई दिल्ली

महाशय,

हमारे स्कूल के लड़के आपका कारखाना देखना चाहते हैं ताकि अपने साधारण ज्ञान को बढ़ा सकें। यदि आप उनको इस की अनुमति दें तो मैं आप का आभारी हूंगा। कृपया दिन तथा समय की भी सूचना दें।

        धन्यवाद

        आपका
        ईश्वर दत्त (प्रधानाध्यापक)

To

    The Manager,
    Modern Baeries,
    New Delhi

Dear Sir,

Our school boys are desirous of visiting your factory so to increase their general knowledge. I shall be grateful if you allow them to do so. Kindly inform about the day and time of the visit. Thanks.

        Yours faithfully

        Headmaster.

[II] Letter to bookseller

२३ भगतसिंह रोड़
आदर्श नगर
दिल्ली
६-३-१९७८

सेवा में,
    व्यवस्थापक
    पीकाक पबलीकेशनस
    नई दिल्ली

महाशय,

कृपया निम्नलिखित पुस्तकें ऊपर लिखे पते पर वी०पी०पी० द्वारा शीघ्र भिजबा दें, आपकी अति कृपा होगी।

१ गबन—प्रेमचन्द
२ कामायनी—जयशंकरप्रसाद

आपका
अशोक कुमार

To
    The Manager,
    Peacock Publications,
    New Delhi

Dear Sir,

Kindly send the under-mentioned books to me on the above address by V.P.P. as early as possible. I shall be grateful to you for this.

1. Gabban—Premchand
2. Kamayani—Jayashankar Prasad

Yours faithfully,
Ashok Kumar.

[III] Letter to friend

२४ भगतसिंह रोड़
नई दिल्ली
९-३-१९७८

प्रिय महेन्द्र,

    तुम्हें यह जान कर बहुत खुशी होगी कि अगले मँगलवार मेरी मंगनी होने जा रही है। इस अवसर पर तुम्हारा यहां आना बहुत अच्छा होगा। कृपया निश्चित दिन प्रातः काल ही यहाँ पहुंच जाना।

तुम्हारा मित्र
देवेन्द्र कुमार

Dear Mahendar,

You will be glad to know that next Tuesday I am going to be engaged. Your presence on this auspicious occasian will be very pleasing. Please reach here on the appointed day in the morning itself.

Yours friendly.

[IV] Application for Service

सेवा में,

>श्रीमान् प्रिन्सिपल महोदय,
>किरोड़ीमल कालेज
>देहली

श्रीमान् जी,

समाचारपत्रों में विज्ञापन से मुझे पता चला है कि आप के कालेज में एक हिन्दी अध्यापक की आवश्यकता है। उसी पद के लिए मैं अपनी सेवाएँ पेश करता हूं।

अपनी योग्यता के विषय में मैं यह कहना चाहता हूं कि मैंने इसी वर्ष हिन्दी में M.A. प्रथम श्रेणी में पास किया। यही नहीं दिल्ली विश्वविद्यालय में मैं प्रथम रहा हूं। इससे पहले बी० ए० (हानर्स) की परीक्षा भी आपके कालेज से प्रथम श्रेणी में पास की थी।

जहाँ तक मेरे स्वभाव का प्रश्न है आप स्वयं ही मुझे बहुत अच्छी प्रकार से जानते हैं क्योंकि मैं सदा आप के आधीन शिक्षा प्राप्त करता रहा हूं।

मैं एक कुलीन घराने का २३ वर्षीय युवक हूं और मेरा स्वास्थ्य इतना अच्छा है कि मैं कड़ी-से-कड़ी मेहनत से भी नहीं घबराता। मुझे पूर्ण आशा है कि मैं अपने काम से आपको पूर्ण रूप से सन्तुष्ट रख सकूंगा।

यदि कृपया आप एक बार मुझे अपने साथ काम करने का सौभाग्य प्रदान करें तो आप की अति कृपा होगी।

धन्यवाद

आपका विश्वासपात्र
अशोक कुमार

Dear Sir,

Having come to know from advertisement in the newspapers that there is a vacancy of Hindi teacher in your college, I offer my services for the same post.

Regarding my qualifications I have to say I passed my M.A. (Hindi) this year is first division. Not only this, I topped the successful candidates in the University of Delhi. Before that I had passed my B.A. (Hons.) examination in first division from your college.

An far as my manners are concerned, you are well aware of me as I have always got my education as your student.

I belong to a good-mannered family and am a 23-year-old youngman with such a good health that I never tire of hard work. I have full faith that I shall be able to satisfy you with my work.

If you kindly give me a chance of work under you, I shall be grateful to you for that.

yours faithfully

[V] Son's letter to father

पूज्य पिताजी,

सादर प्रणाम !

मैं यहाँ २५ तारीख को सकुशल पहुंच गया था । मेरे सारे सहपाठी और अध्यापकगण पचमढ़ी के दृश्य देखकर बहुत खुश हैं । हम लोगों के लिए होटल में रहने का अच्छा प्रबन्ध हो गया है । कल से हम अपना काम यहाँ शुरू करेंगे ।

बाकी सब समाचार ठीक है और आप किसी प्रकार की चिन्ता करें । माता जी को मेरी ओर से प्रणाम कहें ।

आपका आज्ञाकारी पुत्र
महेन्द्र

Respected father,

I reached here on 25th quite all right. All my classmates and teachers were very happy to see sights in Pachmarhi. Good arrangement has been made for our stay in hotel. We will begin our work tomorrow.

Rest is all O.K. Please do not have any anxiety over this. Kindly pay my respects to repected mother.

Yours obediently,
Mahendar

[VI] Sending subscription to paper

व्यवस्थापक,
नवभारत टाईम्ज
नई दिल्ली

महाशय,

मैं अपना वार्षिक चन्दा मनि आर्डर द्वारा आपको भेज रहा हूं कृपया मुझे अगले मास की पहली तारीख से नवभारत टाइम्ज भिजवाने का प्रबन्ध करें । आप की अति कृपा होगी ।

धन्यवाद

आपका
अशोक

दिनांक—१२-३-१९७८

Dear Sir,

I am sending you the yearly subscription for Navbharat Times by moneyorder. Kindly start sending me your paper from the first of the next month. I shall be grateful for this.

Thanks.

Yours faithfully

LESSON 29

Conversation

(बातचीत)

[I] With doctor

मरीज	डाक्टर, मैं बीमार हूं, मुझे दवा दो
Patient	Doctor, I am ill, give me medicine
डाक्टर	क्या तकलीफ है ?
Doctor	What is the trouble ?
मरीज	मुझे कल रात से ज्वर है
Patient	I am having fever since last night
डाक्टर	क्या सर्दी भी लगी है ?
Doctor	Did you feel cold ?
मरीज	हाँ, कुछ कुछ लगी थी मगर अब नहीं है
Patient	Yes, a little cold but it is not now
डाक्टर	ठीक है, यह दवा लो और तीन तीन घंटे बाद खाना
Doctor	All right, here is the medicine, take this every three hours.
मरीज	धन्यवाद, कितने पैसे दूं
Patient	Thans, what is the fee ?
डाक्टर	दो रुपये
Doctor	Two rupees.

[II] With teacher

शिक्षक	तुम्हारा क्या नाम है ?
Teacher	What is your name ?
विद्यार्थी	मैं महेन्द्र हूं
Student	I am Mahendar
शिक्षक	तुम किस कक्षा में पढ़ते हो ?
Teacher	In which class do you read ?
विद्यार्थी	मैं बी. ए. प्रथम वर्ष में हूं
Student	I am in B.A. first year
शिक्षक	तुम्हारे पिता जी का क्या नाम है ?
Teacher	What is the name of your father ?
विद्यार्थी	श्री ईश्बर दत्त
Student	Shri Ishwar Datt
शिक्षक	तुम कहाँ रहते हो और तुम्हारे पिताजी क्या करते हैं ?
Teacher	Where do you live and what is your father ?
विद्यार्थी	हम नई दिल्ली रहते हैं और मेरे पिताजी पत्रकार हैं
Student	We live in New Delhi and my father is a journalist
शिक्षक	ठीक, फिर तो तुम अखबार खूब पढ़ते होंगे
Teacher	Well, then you must be reading lot of newspapers
विद्यार्थी	जी नहीं, पुस्तकों से फुरसत ही नहीं मिलती

Student	No Sir, I hardly get time from reading books
शिक्षक	फिर भी तुम्हें सामान्य ज्ञान की ओर ध्यान देना चाहिये
Teacher	Even then you should pay attention to general knowledge
विद्यार्थी	जी हाँ, मैं भविष्य में ध्यान रखूगा
Student	Yes Sir, I shall keep this in mind in future.

[III] Among Friends

राम	श्याम, कहो भाई, तुम्हारी छुट्टियाँ कब हो रही हैं ?
Ram	Hellow Shyam, when do your vacations start ?
श्याम	हमारी छुट्टियाँ पहली जनवरी से हूंगी
Shyam	Our vacations start from January?
राम	इस बार छुट्टियों में कहाँ जाना है ?
Ram	Where are you going during these holidays ?
श्याम	भई, इस बार तो मैं अपने गाँव जाऊंगा
Shyam	Friend, this time I will go to my village
राम	छोड़ो भी, गांव में क्या रखा है ?
Ram	Damn it, what is there in the village ?

श्याम	क्यों, मेरे माता पिता हैं, भाई बन्धु हैं, मुझे उन के साथ रहने में बहुत आनन्द आता है.
Shyam	Why, my parents and other relations live there. I enjoy so much living with them.
राम	हट भी, मां बाप के पास गांव में क्या मिलेगा ? चलो इस बार दिल्ली घूम आयें
Ram	Leave it, what is there with your parents in the village. Let us this time make a trip to Delhi
श्याम	नहीं नहीं, दिल्ली बड़ा नगर है, बहुत खर्च होता है, मेरे पास इतना धन नहीं है
Shyam	No, No, Delhi is a big city and very expensive. I do not have money.
राम	भई, जब मैं तुम्हारे साथ हूं तो तुम्हें पैसे की चिन्ता क्यों है ?
Ram	Friend, when I am with you, you need not worry about money.
श्याम	नहीं भाई, मैं पहले ही तुम पर बहुत भार डाल चुका हूं अब और नहीं
Shyam	No brother, I have already given you enough trouble, now no more

राम	कोई परवाह नहीं, मैं सीटें बुक करवा रहा हूं और कुछ नहीं जानता, तुम्हें मेरे साथ चलना ही पड़गा
Ram	Never mind, I am booking seats. I know nothing, you will have to go with me.

LESSON 30
Translation
(अनुवाद)

(१) भारत एक बहुत बड़ा देश है और संसार के पुराने देशों में एक माना जाता है । यह कन्याकुमारी से हिमालय के उस छोर तक फैला हुआ हैं । है इस देश का सब से बड़ा गुण यह है कि यहाँ कई जातियों के लोग मिल जुल कर प्रेम से रहते हैं । शायद यही कारण है कि इतने हमलों के भार सहने पर भी यह अडिग खड़ा है जब कि इससे कम भार सहने वाले कई देश इस धरती से लोप हो चुके हैं ।

India is a very vast country and is considered to be one of the antique auntries. It is spread over from Cape Comarin to the other end of the Himalayas. The greatest quality of this country is that here people of different communities live together in peace. Perhaps this is the reason that in spite of taking the load of so many attacks, India stands unmoved while many other countries which had to undergo much lesser rigours have vanished from the face of the earth.

(२) दिल्ली भारत की राजधानी है । यह बहुत पुराना नगर है और अभी तक इसमें पुराने समय के अवशेष मिलते हैं । यह इतना सुन्दर नगर है कि एक बार यहाँ आ जाने पर फिर

कहीं जा बसने को मन नहीं करता। इस नगर की संस्कृति में कुछ ऐसा खिंचाव है कि बरबस यही मुंह से निकलता है—कौन जाए ग़ालिब दिल्ली की गलियाँ छोड़के ?

Delhi is the capital of India. It is an old city and till now we can see the remains of very antique times. This is such a beautiful city that once one comes in he never thinks of leaving it to settle elsewhere. In the culture of this city there is some such thing that we are forced to say—leaving away Delhi's streets, Ghalib, where else you will go ?

(३) एक बूढ़े किसान के चार बेटे थे। वह सदा आपस में लड़ते रहते थे। बाप ने उन्हें बहुत समझाया कि देखो तुम्हारी आपस की लड़ाई से तुम्हारा और वंश का बड़ा अहित होगा। परन्तु उन पर इसका कोई प्रभाव नहीं पड़ा।

किसान एक दिन बीमार पड़ गया। उसे अपने बेटों में झगड़ों के कारण बड़ी चिन्ता थी। उसने सबको पास बुलाया और पतली-पतली लकड़ियों का एक गट्ठा लाने को कहा।

किसान ने सबसे पहले बड़े बेटे को और उसके बाद बारी-बारी से दूसरे को कहा कि इस गट्ठे को बीच में से तोड़ दो। सभी भाई इस काम में असफल रहे।

किसान ने उन्हें गट्ठा खोलने को कहा और उसमें से लकड़ी निकालकर सबको एक-एक दे दी। उसने उन लकड़ियों को तोड़ने को कहा जोकि बिना देर के सब ने कर डाला।

इस पर किसान ने उन्हें समझाया कि इकट्ठी रहती हुई लकड़ियों को कोई नहीं तोड़ सकता जबकि अकेली की हुई झट से टूट गईं । यही तुम्हारा हाल होगा यदि तुम लड़ते रहोगे और अलग-अलग हो जाओगे तो समाज तुम्हें नष्ट कर देगा ।

An old farmer had four sons. They always quarrelled with one another The father counselled them many a time that this quarrel will bring upon you and your family a great doom, but this did not have any effect on them.

The farmer one day fell ill. He was greatly worried over the disunity among his sons. He called all of them and asked them to bring him a bundle of fire sticks.

The farmer asked first the oldest and then the other sons one by one to break the bundle in two. All the brothers failed to do so.

The farmer then asked them to untie the bundle and then he gave each of his son one fire stick. He asked them to break it which all did in no time.

Upon this the farmer advised them that the sticks when they were united, could not be broken while when untied broke so easily, The same will happen to them if they continued quarrelling and separate one from the other. The society will then break them.

(4) मनुष्य के जीवन में सबसे अच्छा समय बच्चपन है । इस आयु में किसी प्रकार की चिन्ता नहीं होती, माता-पिता तथा अन्य लोगों से प्यार मिलता है. अच्छी चीजें खाने को तथा अच्छे कपड़े पहनने को मिलते हैं और जहाँ तक हो सके सब आराम देते हैं चाहे इसके लिए उन्हें कुछ कष्ट ही क्यों न उठाना पड़े । कोई मां-बाप बच्चों के लिए पत्थर कूटते हैं, कोई बोझा ढोते हैं फिर भी जो जिससे बन पड़ता है अपनी संतान के लिये करता है जिससे उसे आराम मिले ।

In man's life, childhood is the best of times. In this age there is no worry, parents and other people show love. give good things to eat and good clothes to wear and as far as possible provide for full comfort even though they have to bear difficulties for this. For their children some parents break stones, some carry loads, even then whatever is possible is done so that the progeny can live in comfort

(5) पुस्तकें भी विचित्र उपहार हैं । जब हमारे जीवन में हर ओर से दुःख के बादल घिर आते हैं, तो पुस्तकें ही सच्चे मित्रों की भांति हमें तसल्ली देती हैं । जब अन्य प्रिय मित्र तथा सम्बन्धी हमारा बुरे समय में साथ छोड़ देते हैं, पुस्तकें हमारा साथ देती हैं । वे हमारा साहस बढ़ाती हैं और कष्टों पर विजय पाना सिखाती हैं । पुस्तकें मनुष्य के हजारों वर्षों के अनथक प्रयत्नों का प्रमाण हैं । फिर भी सभी पुस्तकें अच्छी नहीं होतीं । हमें पढ़ने के लिए केवल अच्छी पुस्तकें ही लेनी चाहियें ।

Books are strange gifts. When in our lives hover the dark clouds of distress, then books like true friends provide us consolation. When other dear friends and relations leave as in ill times, books stick to us. They increase our courage and teach us how to win over difficulties. Books are the result of man's continuous work of thousands of years. Even then all books are not good. We should chooseonly good books for reading.

VOCABULARY

House, household and garden
(घर, घरेलू तथा बाग सम्बन्धी)

House	घर	ghar
Room	कमरा	Kamra
Door	दरवाजा	darwaja
Window	खिड़की	Khirki
Ceiling	छत	chhat
Floor	फर्श	farash
Staircase	जीना, सिढ़ियां	zina, seerihyan
Storey	मंजिल	manzil
Building	इमारत, भवन	imarat, bhavan
Basement	तहखाना	tehkchana
Bathroom	स्नानालय गुसलखांना	sananalay
Kitchen	रसोइघर	rasoyighar
Diningroom	भोजनालय	bhojanalay
Bedroom	सोने का कमरा	sone ka kamra
Courtyard	आंगन, सहन	aangan, sehan
Drawing room	बैठक	baithak
Ground flour	नीचे की मंजिल	neeche ki manzil

First floor	पहली मंज़िल	pehli manzil
Lavatory	शौचालय, टट्टी	souchalay, tatti
Verandah	बरामदा	baramda
Wood, timber	लकड़ी	lakri
Wall	दीवार	deewar
Ventilator	रोशनदान	roshandan
Door-frame	चौखट	chaukhat
Brick	ईंट	eent
Lime	चूना	choona
Glass	शीशा	sheesha
Lock	ताला	tala
Bolt	चटखनी	chatakhni
Handle	दस्ता	dasta
Nail	कील	keel
Padlock	ताला	tala
Peg	खूंटी	khunti
Vessel	बर्तन	bartan
Oven, hearth	अंगीठी	angithi
Almirah	अल्मारी	almari
Coal	कोयला	koyla
Fire	आग	aag
Firewood	जलने की लकड़ी	jalana ki lakri
Spoon	चमच	chamach

Plate	थाली	thali
Cup	प्याला	piyala
Bowel (big)	कटोरा	katoraa
Bowel (small)	कटोरी	katoree
Bucket	बालटी	balti
Crockery	चीनी का सामान	chini ka saman
Dish	प्याली	piyali
Filter, sieve	छाननी	channee
Forceps	चिमटा	chimta
Fuel	ईंधन	eendhan
Branch [tree]	शाखा	shaakha
Bud	कली	kali
Bunch	गुछा	guchha
Bush	झाड़ी	jhari
Creeper	बेल	bel
Flower	फूल	phool
Rose	गुलाब	gulab
Garden	बाग	baag
Gardener	माली	mali
Grass	घास	ghass
Hedge	घेरे की झाड़ी	gheray ki jhari
Leaf	पत्ता	pata
Cupboard	आलमारी (दीवान में)	almari

Cinder	अंगारा	aangara
Cauldran	कड़ाही	karahi
Canister	कनस्तर	kanastar
Comb	कंघी	kanghi
Fork	कांटा	kaanta
Pastry-board	चकला	chakla
Mat	चटाई	chattai
Stove	चूल्हा	choolha
Stick	छड़ी	chhhari
Umbrella	छाता	chhata
Broom	झाड़ू	jharu
Swing	झूला	jhoola
Basket	टोकड़ी	tokri
Lid	ढकना	dhakna
Pillow	तकिया	takia
Balance	तराज़ू	tarazu
Wire	तार	tar
Quilt	रजाई	rajai
mirror	शीशा	sheesha
Match box	दियासलाई डिबी	diyasilai dibi
Match-stick	दियासलाई तिली	,, teeli
Saucepan	देगची	degchi

thread	धागा	dhaga
bedstead	पलंग	palang
door mat	पायदन	payadan
spittoon	पीकदान	peekdan
flower-vase	फूलदान	phooldan
wick	बत्ती	bati
button	बटन	batan
churner	मथनी	mathni
candle	मोमबती	mombati
rope	रस्सा	rassa
string	रस्सी	rassi
cabinet	कपड़े टागंने की अल्मारी	kapre ki almari
phial	शीशी	sneeshi
soop	साबुन	sabun
soapcase	साबुनदानां	sabundani
jug	सुराही	surahi
needle	सूई	sui
bark	छाल	chhal
skin	छिलका	chhilka
root	जड़	jar
pollen	नोरा	neera
thorn	कांटा	kaanta
teak	सागवान	saagwan
branch	शाखा	shakha
fibre	रेशा	resha

juice	रस	ras
seed	बीज	beej
graft	कलम	kalam
bud	कली	kali
stone	गुठली	guthli
pulp	गूदा	gooda
gum	गोंद	gond
palm	ताड़	taar

Colours

bright	चमकीला	chamkeela
black	काला	kala
blue	नीला	neela
brown	भूरा	bhoora
dark	गहरा	gehra
green	हरा	hara
golden	सुनहरी	sunehri
grey	सलेटी भूरी	saleti bhoora
indigo	बैंगनी	bengni
light	हल्का	halka
orange	नारंजी	naranji
pink	गुलाबी	gulabi
pale	पीला कपूरी	peela, kapoori
red	लाल	lal
white	सफेद	safed
yellow	पीला	peela

Flowers and Vegetables

फूल तथा सब्जियां

Jasmine	चमेली	Chameli
Marigold	गेंदा	genda
Rose	गुलाब	gulab
Lotus	कमल	kamal
Lily	कमलिनी	kamalini
Pandanus	केतकी	ketki
Chrysenthemum	गुलदाउरी	guldaudi
Touch-me-not	गुलमेंहदी	gulmehndi
Daisy	गुलबाहर	gulbahar
Magnolia	चम्पा	Champa
Narcissus	नरगिस	nargis
Oleander	कनेर	kaner
Cobra flower	नागमिका	naagmika
poppy	पोस्त	post
Sweet violef	बनफश	banafsha
Ginger	अदरक	adrak
potato	आलू	aloo
tamarind	इमली	imli
Cucumber	ककड़ी	kakri
Jack fruit	कटहल	Kathal
Pumpkin	कद्दू सीताफल	Kaddoo, sitaphal
Bitter gourd	करेला	kerela
Red pumpkin gourd	काशीफल	kashiphal

Mushroom	कुकुरमुत्ता	kukurmuta
Lime	नीबू	neebu
Cucumber	खीरा	kheera
Citrom	गलगल	galgal
Carrot	गाजर	gajar
Luffa	घिया, तुराई	ghiya turai
Citron	चकोतरा	chakotra
Luffa gourd	चिकनी तोरी	chikni tori
sugar beet	चुकन्दर	chukander
amaranthus	चौलाई	cholai
crab apple	जंगली सेब	jangli seb
coriander	धनिया	dhanie
Coconut	नारियल	narial
Lemon	नीबू	neenbu
Cauliflower	फूलगोभी	phulghobi
Spinach	पालक	palak
Mint	पुदीना	pudeena
Onion	प्याज	piyaz
Cabbage	बन्दगोभी	bandgobhi
brinjal	बैंगन	baingan
Lady's finger	भिंडी	bhindi
pea	मटर	mattar
Chili	मिरच	mirch
Radish	मूली	mooli
garlic	लहसुन	Lehsun
turnip	शलजम	shaljam
Lettuce	सलरा	salad

Sago	साबूदाना	sabudana
Bean	सेम	sem
Tomato	टमाटर	tamatar
Drum stick	सहजन	sahjan
Aniseed	सौंफ	saunf
Arum	अरबी	arabee
Asfoctida	हींग	heeng
Capsicum	हरी मिर्च	harimirch
Sauce	चटनी	chatnee
Vinegar	सिरका	sirka

Fruits and spices

(फल तथा मसाले)

Apple	सेब	seb
Banana	केला	kelaa
Berry	बेर	ber
Custard apple	शरीफा	sharifa
Grape	अंगूर	angoor
guava	अमरुद	amrood
jambu	जामुन	jamun
mango	आम	aam
melon	तरबूज	tarbooz
mulberry	शहतूत	shahtoot
orange	संतरा	santra
papaye	पपीता	papeeta

peach	आड़ू	aaroo
pear	नाशपाती	nashpatee
pineapple	अनानास	anaanaas
plantain	केला	kela
pomegranate	अन्नार	annaar
fig	अंजीर	anjir
plum, bokhara	आलू बुखारा	aaloo bukhara
plum	अलूचा	aaloocha
sugarcane	ईख, गन्ना	eekh, ganaa
musk melon	खरबूजा	kharbooza
cucumber	खीरा	kheera
carrot	गाजर	gajjar
citron	चकोतरा	chakotra
sapodilla	चीकू	cheekoo
black berry	जामुन	jamun
betel	पान	paan
grawia asiatica	फालसा	falsa
corn ear	भुट्टा	bhutta
malta	मालटा	malta
sweet cherry	मीठी चेरी	meethi cheri
mosambi	मौसमी	mausami
lichi	लीची	lichi
sweet potato	शकरकंदी	shakar-kandi

sago	साबूदाना	saboodana
waternut	सिंघाड़ा	singhara
Almond	बादाम	badaam
betelnut	सुपारी	supari
cashewnut	काजू	kaaju
coconut	नारियल	naariyal
currants	मुनक्का, दाख	munakkaa-dakh
dates	खजूर	khajoor
dry fruit	सूखा मेवा	sookha meva
fig	अंजीर	anjeer
pistachio	पिस्ता	pista
raisins	मुनक्का, किशमिश	munakkaa-kishmish
rind	छिलका	chilakaa
walnut	अखरोट	akhroat
stone	गुठली	guthlee
seeds	बीज	beej
groundnut	मूंगफली	moongphali
poppy	पोस्त	post
coconut	नारियल	nariyal
pinus gerardiana	चिलगोजा	chilgoza
apricot	खुबानी	khubani
currant	किशमिश	kishmish
aniseed	सौंफ	saunf
asfoetida	हींग	heeng

cardamom (big)	डोडा	doda
cardamom (small)	ईलायची	ilaayachi
cassia leaf	तेजपत्र	tejpatra
cloves	लौंग	laung
coriander	धानिया	dhaniya
turminseed	जीरा	jeera
fenugreek	मेथी	maithi
ginger	सौंठ	saunth
garlic	लहसुन	lehsun
mustard	राई	raa-ee

Foods and Driuks
खाने-पीने की वस्तुएँ

Grain	अनाज	anaaj
flour	आटा	aata
pulses	दालें	dalain
pickle	अचार	achar
arrowroot	अराऋट	araroot
curry	कढ़ी	karhi
coffee	काफी	kafi
tea	चाय	chai
meat	मांस	mans
minced meat	कीमा	keema
mutton	बकरी का मांस	bakri ka mans

pork	सुअर का मांस	suar ka mans
chicken	मुर्गे का मांस	murge ka mans
beef	गाय का मांस	gaya ka mans
comfit	इलायची दाना	ilaichi dana
ice-cream	कुलफी	kulfi
wheat	गेहूँ	gaihoon
butter	माखन	maakhan
ghee	घी	ghee
gram	चना	chana
cake	चपाती	chapati
sugar	चीनी	chini
bran	चोकर	chokar
millet	ज्वार बाजरा	jawar, bajra
lunch	दोपहर का खाना	dopehr ka khana
break fast	नाशता	nashta
supper	रात का खाना	raat ka khana
oat	जई	jaiae
barley	जौ जब	jao
broth	शोरब	shorba